Berry

For

f r a g i l e

a memoir

Jeffrey Thomson

Excerpt/s from "Questions of Travel" from POEMS by Elizabeth Bishop. Copyright © 2011 by The Alice H. Methfessel Trust. Publisher's Note and compilation copyright © 2011 by Farrar, Straus and Giroux, LLC. Reprinted by permission of Farrar, Straus and Giroux, LLC.

Pieces of this book previously appeared, often in very different forms, in other venues. I am grateful to the editors and publishers of the following books and journals for their support:

Ecological Poetry: A Critical Introduction, ISLE, Gulf Coast, Birdwatching in Wartime, Concord Saunterer, Watershed, and *Isotope.*

ISBN 978-0-9908047-2-7

Printed in the United States of America

RED MOUNTAIN PRESS

Santa Fe, New Mexico

www.redmountainpress.us

Acknowledgements

The National Endowment for the Arts, the Pennsylvania Council on the Arts, the Maine Arts Commission, Chatham University, and, particularly, the University of Maine at Farmington all provided material support during the time I was working on this book. For that help I am particularly grateful. As for individuals, there are too many people who need acknowledgement for their assistance and the help they have given me in the years it has taken to complete this work, so a smaller number than I would like will need to stand in synecdoche. Sherod Santos, Lynne McMahon, and Trish Roberts-Miller were all there at the germination stage and deserve special acknowledgement. Huge thanks are due to Christian Barter who read repeated drafts and helped me orchestrate and construct any kind of meaning out of this cacophony. Bill Roorbach gave me a generous and insightful reading of the manuscript at a critical moment as well. Patrick Thomas helped me understand my own process and Drew Barton has been invaluable in helping me think about trees. Chelsea Browning-Bohannah, Breanna Dawn Deluca, and Max Eyes did serious yeoman labor helping me prepare this manuscript. Many thanks are due, too, to Susan Gardner for believing in this book. I am also grateful to Dave, who first went with me to Costa Rica, and Tony, who accompanied me first to Europe. Luis Torres has been my guide and my friend for more than a decade and deserves much of the credit for things I pretend to know about Costa Rica. I am very grateful to the doctors and nursing staff of Tufts Medical Center and the Hypertrophic Cardiomyopathy Center for keeping me alive to write this. And, finally, my parents, my sister, and most of all Jennifer Anne, and Julian—they all deserve special thanks for letting me go and wander around the wild world writing about what I saw there. Bless you all.

for Julian

Continent, city, country, society:
the choice is never wide and never free.
And here, or there . . . No. Should we have stayed at home,
wherever that may be?

~ Elizabeth Bishop
"Questions of Travel"

I.

In the seventh hour of my ascent I begin to weep. There has been nothing but a road rising before me for hours. The wet, scrubby rainforest of the low Cartago mountains has given way to twisted trees and the stunted *páramo* of the high plateau of Talamanca and a long, red line of pain has run the length of my legs and settled in my ass. The yoke of my shoulders carries a dull bone-ache. It hurts horribly to breathe. The wheels of my mountain bike spin and spin—a slow churn up the road through the air ever cooling. A green mist of cloud-filled trees flanks the long road that climbs and climbs. My tires sizzle on the road as I rise through the remains of a late rain. Ahead of me the summit of *Cerro de la Muerte*—the mountain of death—is somewhere in the mist, and then the tears come and do not cease. I am not crying. I am not sobbing. The tears just seep from me and do not stop, the water of my body leaking from some deep well.

§

Two weeks we had been in Costa Rica, me and my friend Dave, mountain biking and in that time we had ridden up the huge, green hills of the *Parque Nacional Braulio Carrillo* and down their slopes through the mist in a hiss of air. Up we went into the sway of the clouds against the trees, up inside the sky where the mountains live folded back against themselves in blankets of avocado and jade and the charcoal of old volcanoes humped up in the bed of the air. From the Pacific slope into the Atlantic, climbing up one watershed and descending another. Up, up, up into the hills—long climbs and then the sweet flush of the descent coming down the other side into fields of aloe and farms where ornamental plants relax beneath sheets of black mesh, hiding from the potent sun.

We coasted down to the Caribbean, the water rough and chopped with the wind coming up out of the east, and then along beach roads, past the empty hotels ringed with coconut palms and the Rastafarian tri-color. We hung out with a collection of very serious surfers in a town just kilometers from Nicaragua and smoked a little of their dope but refused the gift bag they offered us, which was lucky, because when the police stopped us the next day as we rode back north we were clean as morning. We rode into the rainforest near Cahuita where the white-faced capuchin monkeys leapt from tree to tree in a kind of aerial ballet while orange-streaked-jade iguanas the size of collies sat in patches of sunlight and basked in Jurassic ease.

I was comfortable in the saddle and the bike felt like the way to see the Costa Rica I wanted to see, the backroads of small and intimate country: the wild ruckus of the rainforest stretching out over a headland and running down to an immaculate sea, the whole Tarzan-fantasy of it, yes, but also the small farms and the daily life. Houses of pink pastel stucco tucked into tiny groves of banana and papaya where black-haired children chased soccer balls and walked the red-dirt roads to the tin-roofed *pulpería* for treats in the afternoon. The farmer with his tall rubber boots and the machete on his hip driving a Brahma bull and a cart loaded down with palm fronds to re-thatch his roof. The man galloping through the surf as he forces his horse down the shore toward his home on the coast near Cahuita. Gigantic colonies of bromeliads lining the branches of kapok trees—the trees rowdy and occupied as living hotels. Acres of banana and fields of rice. Toucans.

I wanted to know the place, to become intimate with it. I wanted to come away fluent. That wasn't what happened, exactly.

§

When we first landed in Costa Rica it was twilight, the sun already behind the coastal mountains to the west, the sky a ripe burn along the peaks surrounding the city, fading to deep indigo in the east. We climbed off the plane onto the tarmac and into humid air thick with lanolin and octane. With the large corrugated hangar above us, all of the passengers descended the ramp into an open-air immigration line and waited. It was almost night by the time I passed through to baggage claim and picked up my luggage, more than the normal suitcases and duffels. I found the box that held my mountain bike and struggled to move with it through the crowd towards customs. Sliding it across the concrete floor was like shoving a mule along a muddy path. Awkward and tipsy, it suffered my efforts only to slam to the floor again and again. Everyone gave me a wide berth.

Then the lights went out. A sudden, quonset darkness. We stood there, waiting for the power and the lights to return. A darkness rich and charged. We waited. People, shadowed against the last of the visible sky, thronged into the hall. No one stopped; they filled up the arched dark. I stood still and waited. The lights stayed out. The hall stayed dark. The sky lost the last of its light as the people flowed around us, unconcerned. The air was sweltering and tangy with sweat and the odor of cigarettes. The whole thing felt like a fever dream.

We finally shuffled through customs in the pungent dark with no acknowledgement from anyone. Maybe they couldn't see us in the dark. Long-haired Americans. Maybe they just didn't care. We slipped out, finally, to the curb and found a van the color of blotchy mold and rusted through at the wheel-wells to take us into San José. Along the way I lost my hiking boots and backpack full of clothes. I set them down in the dark and never found them again.

§

In the cathedral, that miraculous anthill of gilt and carving that lives at the center of town, in a small alcove off the nave, there is a carved wooden Christ that is dark from candle black. He's been floating in the rich smoke above the small lake of votive light for hundreds of years. The perfection of his crucifixion was long ago engraved into the whorls and loops and ridges of his cross—like the fingerprints of God on the wood. It feels dramatic and full of pain, the agony of the real, even now as these new, electric votives turn a burned light upon his smoked, black form. All the more, the strange crimson wig of *ñucchu* flowers he wears—such odd, fuchsia curls draped on his sagging head—seems to highlight his suffering. Within the God-made flesh that this carved Christ represents, what has burnt away there on the cross is the human form, the brute body, until only the something beyond

14

this world is left. The remains of the man who went into himself there on the cross and didn't return.

§

So after two weeks of riding, we returned to San José, the country's capitol that sits in the central valley rimmed by high mountains, and rode up to Cartago. We would use Cartago as a staging area for an attempt on *Cerro de la Muerte*, one of the highest peaks in Costa Rica. A mountain named for those who have died on it, including a plane of eleven missionaries from Honduras that crashed early in the 20th century. They are buried there up among the clouds. Their grave markers sit at close to 3,000 meters on the Pan-American Highway that ascends and ascends and ascends, and is sometimes not really a highway but rather a trick of the light, an asphalt niche in the side of the mountain that you can climb and climb until climbing is all that is possible anymore.

We returned to the center of the country and I began to prepare for my ride. Dave, my friend, had had enough; enough of the bike, enough climbing, enough backroads nostalgia, and had rented a car. He was tired and thought what I wanted to do—ride up the mountain and over along the Pan-American Highway—was goddamn foolish. That's the nicest way to say it. He was done; he was taking the road north to the coast at Puntarenas and then driving south along the shore. The plan was for us to meet on the beach in Dominical in two days time—that's how long I guessed it would take for me to ride south over *Cerro de la Muerte* and down into the valley of San Isidro and then up again over the coastal mountains and into the sweet relief of Dominical—the long sweep of sand and the sea and the sun.

I had trained for weeks getting ready for this trip back home in Colorado; I lived at 7,000 feet and had skied and climbed nearly every day for the better part of half a year. Before the trip I put in a lot of hours in the saddle, and in two weeks in the country I had already ridden what I thought were huge climbs. I thought I was ready. I wasn't. There was a line I had yet to cross, an edge to this world of everyday toil and fret, a place I had yet to see, perhaps because it can't be seen.

So now, in the brightening morning in Cartago—old, colonial town of ruin and bougainvillea—I say goodbye to Dave as he gets in his rental car, his bike disassembled and clutched in the trunk, and he slides off into the light morning traffic. I ride out of the colonial stonework and gingerbread of the city, a rough and broken town that has seen far better days. The fretwork around the rafters of the houses is peeling and knocked off randomly, at odd angles. Stray bougainvillea throttles fences above small stone patios with sprays of deep purple. Now, as I ride out through the nearly empty, early morning streets past the highway heading back to San José and begin the ascent, the sunlight from the east just touches the top of the Turrialba volcano, the valley still in shadow, and trucks delivering the day's bread and newspapers are my only companions.

My legs churn the first miles easily, up and up into the hills as I leave the city behind. The sun climbs with me as I ascend, the clouds gathering in the distance. Small farms pass by—the corrugated steel roofs painted a scarlet-gone-orange now faded beneath the pounding sun—and often people stop the work they are doing in their gardens or turn on their chairs in the roadside restaurants to stare at me as I pass— slowly, so slowly and always climbing, climbing past gardens of papaya and plantain, the undergrowth of wild impatiens and poor man's umbrella. My bike in its lowest gear. My knees spinning and spinning. Then the steepness increases and often I am standing on the pedals, pushing and sweating, my heart thudding in my chest and neck. The road narrows and flows around corner after corner. The valley farms give way to mountain driveways leading to hidden houses and the ramshackle overhangs of the roadside truck stops looking to the Pacific off the right side, or the Caribbean to the left. Soon even they are gone and nothing remains but the road, climbing and climbing and narrowing into the distance.

I ride and I ride. Hour after hour. The road keeps ascending before me like a long, optical illusion, like a Mobius strip forever above me. Long after I am cursing Dave and his goddamn car, cursing my choice to make this climb, long after I want to turn my bike around and with relief flow back down the mountain like the wind to San José, I ride. My legs pump, my breath huffs, the road climbs, and I ride. I have no choice. There is nowhere for me to go. Dave is gone. He has taken the car and driven west to Puntarenas and the Pacific coast. I have no way to contact him. The only way is forward and forward means up.

And then I start to weep. After seven hours, I weep like an unending sump flowing out of the hillside. The tears come and come and my eyes are open and emptying and my legs spin. I don't remember much from this point on. I know logically what happens. I know I ride those last hours up into the mist and onto the top of the mountain. I know the road climbs up into the clouds and the cold wind, but I can tell you only a little.

There is a place in the body—a place of pleasure above pain, where both blend together so perfectly that it is impossible to tell the difference between the two— and after seven hours I find it. This is the dark center, the empty hole at the core of our daily life, like the eye of the hurricane or the calm center of a vortex, the open secret and the necessary lie. Despite what that vision of Christ on his cross would say, it is not a place of spirit. I don't think so at least. It is very physical, not something supernatural, and has everything to do with the body, with our concrete engagement with the world. It is not holy, though it feels that way. This space, this place, it is of the body and of nature. It has something to do with life and everything to do with death.

It has something to do with John Keats, too. Just last night before we began our ascent, in our small hotel room of rough boards and two cots, the soft cooing of the chickens roosting just beyond the wall, beneath a single bare bulb casting a jaundiced light, I read this, the beginning of one of his most famous poems:

> My heart aches, and a drowsy numbness pains
> My sense, as though of hemlock I had drunk,
> Or emptied some dull opiate to the drains
> One minute past, and Lethe-wards had sunk:

That's what I feel like. Like I am bathed in an opiate dream, sun drenched and full of mist at the same time, like I am going down into myself in a sleep of warm clouds turning cold and colder slowly still. I am traveling down a tunnel of my own thoughts and dreams, and rising up and up again into the sky and the thin scrub trees that wear coats of bromeliads and moss, climbing from the green world of summer up into the landscape of death, climbing up into a cemetery. Because this mountain is a cemetery filled with those missionaries and those other forgotten dead who died crossing this tough terrain, climbing up from the green fields and the orchid-warmth of the valleys, out of frangipani and bougainvillea into this world of mist and white. Into this scrubland of low grass and wind. Into the cold. They climbed up and died, exposed and raw. I feel like I may soon join them.

Keats goes on. He wants, he wishes:

> ...for a beaker full of the warm South,
> Full of the true, the blushful Hippocrene,
>   With beaded bubbles winking at the brim,
>   And purple-stained mouth;
> That I might drink, and leave the world unseen,
>   And with thee fade away into the forest dim:

He's talking to bird here, a nightingale. He wants to leave our human world and with that beautiful, hidden bird, fade away into the forest. He hopes for ease and balm and the setting down of care. That's why I came to Costa Rica—for *a beaker full of the warm south*, a blast of sun and green and the easy sway of the warm wind after longs months of white and ice and the tightened muscles of the cold, for birds of great plumage and glorious song—but instead now I find myself floating upwards into the chill wind of what feels like my own mortality. Cars hiss by me—they have been doing so all day. The bromeliads haunt the trees, magenta leaves spotting the dark shadows like odd aerial aloe, with their roots hanging from the branches of a hundred kapoks; I no longer see them. There are clusters of poor man's umbrella rising up beside the gutters, huge parasols. My water bottles are empty—at some point I finish them, but I don't remember taking a drink. What I know is tears, lots of tears. My face has faucets and they are open. I may be dying but I feel an odd sense of peace, a sense of not even being on the bike anymore. I try to stop but my legs keep going. Spinning and spinning. They are no longer in my control. They have become things unto themselves.

So I ride and my legs no longer follow my instructions. The tears run down my face like rain. The pain stops. Its song, which has been with me since shortly after I quit Cartago at six this morning, is gone and in its place hums a wash of white. The road buzzes. The pedals turn themselves and I am free to wander around my own mind. I see my parents, my mother reading in a sunlit window, my father covered in sawdust, sanding a long pine board. I see Jennifer, the woman I left in the States to come and grind my body into a pulp biking the mountains of Costa Rica, her brown hair swept down across her face, her rowdy smile and quick laugh. I see food, plates of *gallo pinto*, steaks dripping butter, glasses of dark, dark beer. I see the pummeling surf of the beach at Cahuita breaking on the dark, volcanic stone. I see banana plantations tunneling off into the distance. I see birds, a glorious churning of color and flash in the dark shadows of the trees, turning and disappearing into gloom like the unknown heart of the rainforest. I don't know how I keep my bike on the road.

§

This carved version of Christ stopped the earthquake, the story says, stopped the rolling of the pitch-pole earth as the low arroyos above the city shed their skins and brimmed with sudden stone. The tremor faded as he was paraded by the priests across the square, as he—*el Señor de los Temblores*, Lord of Earthquakes—was held high above the quaking crowd, with banners of cloud assembling in glory on the ridgelines. The spectacle that calmed the earth, his hatchet face and his black plaited beard, Christ hangdog on the cross, and the terrible need of the gathering crowd: all these details conspire towards the belief that there is something larger than the world. Something beyond us and supernatural. They tell a story that there is a world beyond this world, a world of power and beneficence. That's what the painting sharing the sacristy certainly argues for; it tells the same story of *el Dios herido* (the wounded God) who strokes the roaring earth with clouds and beds it back down in blankets of sun as celebration rises up like a chorus of doves from the crowd assembled in the square.

But out beyond the town, after the quake, where the river slipped its banks and emptied a farmer's agave field that had been colonized by rats, and where walls topped with cactus collapsed in on that same farmer and his wife, something else was happening. Another story was being told. The world was still the world, but it was settling. The world was falling back into itself. Everything built up was coming undone. While trees merely shook and rattled. The adobe bricks returned, *like all flesh,* to the earth from which they were made.

20

§

When Hernán Cortés and his soldiers, acclimated to sea level, crossed the mountains north of here, heading for what later would be named Mexico City but which the natives called Tenochtitlan, they saw St. James riding through the mist, a horseman one-hundred feet tall charging through the volcanic smoke and low clouds. In their delirium, in the face of this alien world, their minds turned back to what they knew, to their version of the civilized world. To form and history and their cities. James was an idol for the Spanish (his remains were found in Galicia in the ninth century): the inspiration of their victory over the Moors, the patron saint of the re-conquest of Spain, a symbol of God's will in motion, a vision sent to show them the true path. Following him they found a trail through the mountains and went on to destroy Tenochtitlan.

§

I ride and I ride, my legs pounding and churning. I ride until I can't ride anymore and then I ride on. I ride until I arrive at the edge of all meaning, where nothing is real. A sense of peace rises up like fog, like a world of limitless nothing, a present absence, an absent presence. I flow through this white world, weeping. I can't see or feel anything concrete. I am *in* a vacuum and I *am* a vacuum. And into that vacuum (and from it, as well) flow images of the world. Because there is nothing there, I guess, my mind, in its necessary attempts to turn that nothing into something, to define and clarify meaning out of nothing, turns to images it can define. Looking into that wide and flowing absence, my mind swerves away and lands on what it knows. I see the burn of sunset above the shadowed mountains around San José; the forever twilight of the rainforest along the *Rio Suerte,* the river of luck, with the water's deep, tannic black reflecting the scattered blue of the sky. I see a burnt black Christ floating above a lake of votive light. A stilled heart at the end of a long tunnel. I smell acrid sweat in a quonset dark.

The monk flagellating himself for hours with thorns ascends into a state of spiritual bliss so like his image of Christ on the cross, the empty self willing to give up its physical shell to a world beyond. Siddhartha Gautama aches for enlightenment under the Bodhi tree on the fortieth day of his fast and enters Nirvana. These are metaphors for eternity and emptiness, a release from the prison of the self. Those in great distress who seek to escape that distress by going deeper into it, by going through it. They go into their pain, inhabit it, in order to move beyond it. That is the feeling Keats longs for in "Ode to a Nightingale," the opiate bliss of extremity and pain. A world beyond *beyond*, a world of green and safety. This place is the edge of our perception, the boundary of our thought, but it is also the world of illusion. This is the draught of the Hippocrene that Keats talks about, the aesthetic fountain of the muses kicked into the world by the hooves of a winged horse. It is the world of poetry. A world where the arias of Verdi come unbidden and you hear them as if sung from all around you, sung by angels from on high. This is the world where everything connects, and distance is eclipsed. This is a world of death *and* life, but it is also the world of image and metaphor. It is the world that is not, but that we wish were true. This is the world of the gauzy tropical island on the far horizon, a beach of white and gold ebbing at your feet. This is the world of the desert mirage, the dark shadows of fruit trees and fresh water that recede ever before you. The world of warmth in the worst blizzard, the voice telling you that the nearby snowbank would be a comfortable place for a rest, warm sleep washing over you. It is a dangerous world, but like all danger, it is ultimately beautiful.

When I finally near the summit of *Cerro de la Muerte,* the wind whips tattered banners of low clouds across the peak where the small white crosses of the eponymous dead crowd a granite marker like some macabre Point-of-Interest. That plane slammed into the hillside from an obscuring cloudbank fifty years ago. One or two of its passengers may have survived for a day or so, watching the gray apparitions dance and vanish across the clouds as they slipped in and out of consciousness until, finally, they all dropped into darkness. Balanced on the rim of two worlds, did they see their loved ones, food in the Public Market in San José, fishing boats of Limon? Or did they, like the conquering Spaniards, see saints and angels?

I cross the mountain of death nine hours after I started and alone. I am consumed. Empty. I stand alone in the cold, white air, exhausted and shaking, with my bike beside me. There is a desolation where my stomach once was and my legs are nearly liquid. The traffic has vanished, leaving me solitary in the face of the wind that has climbed with me, up from the dense heat of the lowlands, up through the misted architecture of the cloud forest to the peak. In the stark *páramo*—that low and rough chusquea grassland that survives in the wind and cold at the top of this mountain in small bunches of grassy shrubs huddling low—amidst the bluster of clouds whipping past, inside the sky and the cold mist that drips from everything solid, I stand briefly alone at the peak of the world looking at the tops of clouds converging on me from two oceans.

That dark center, that peak that is also a valley, that place where presence meets absence, that boundary between worlds where pain gives rise to something beyond itself, where words fail and knowledge meets the end of knowing, that center rewards me with a blank space. A place made of air, whose meanings are so many and so diverse I cannot know exactly of what I speak. It feels like the limit of what I can know, but also, perhaps, the limit of knowability itself: a place both specific and amorphous where pain slips into pleasure, where the scouring of flesh with thorns and the salt-blood becomes rapture, where arias arise from malaria's fever, where a burned-black body holds a still and undamaged heart within its ruins. A place where the body scours the spirit, where enjambment with the world scrapes the self raw.

At the top of the mountain of the dead I find only emptiness and absence, a space where I cannot linger. Mountain valleys drop east down to the Caribbean, all stillness and palm, and west to the wild, deep swell of the Pacific. The road at my feet flows away north, running as far as Alaska, and south to the end of the continent in Chile. This is the *axis mundi*, the center of the world, I think, but here at that center is a gap, an empty space. I can see nothing. In all directions descends whiteness like some sort of gauzy dream. At the end of my efforts there is, in fact, nothing to see—a simple and glorious missing. The clouds surround me in their white breath. The sky gathers at my feet. The air passes coldly through my sweat-damp clothes. Oh yes, it is cold. I am unwelcome and cannot remain.

§

I ride down into the valley of San Isidro de El General more than eleven hours after I began—the city laid out before me in the valley of green and gold, like a welcoming net stretched across the earth as if it could save my life. Down and down and down again with the air warming as I go, the smell of the asphalt and the earth mixing with the occasional hot blast of jasmine or diesel exhaust. Down and down for more than an hour, swinging out around the switchbacks with the huge bulk of the semi-trailers joining me. The city grows larger and larger until it looks like order and history and meaning and life. It looks like everything I need and I flow down into its noise and smoke and light.

The traffic hums and sings as I reenter the human world. The tin roofs and electric wires, the open doors filled with music and the architectural racks of roasting chickens. Women joking and laughing in doorways of lime green and soft orange. Laundry strung out between rooftop windows. TV aerials and the twigs of rebar sticking out from unfinished walls. Children.

In San Isidro de El General, after hauling my bike to the third floor where my hotel room overlooks the mountains I crossed and the red-roofed grid of the city, I sit in a café on the city square—the statues and lawn and the tall palms of that manicured garden spread out before me in a generous welcome—and eat a whole fried fish, the eye facing me empty and flat, and a rich, steaming mound of *gallo pinto,* dark and spotted like the rough fruit of the earth itself. I drink more than several beers. Above the square, in the towering blue of the late afternoon sky, black vultures funnel up and up while at the table beside me two men argue in AMSLAN, vehemently silent.

II.

The next moring early I am back on my bike. Climbing
again. Out of San Isidro, out of the grid of the city, its
precision and the right angles of urban life. I leave the
small homes of plaster and tin, quiet lime paint and
gray-as-ash cinderblock, each house covered in
corrugated red steel and surrounded by walls built to
hide it from the street. The deep gutters that catch the
rainy season. I leave the tire shops and the *panaderias*,
their doors open and smelling of sugar and flour, the
racks of pastries   like small whirlpools. I pass a
department store spotted with a garish rooster logo—a
swirling red cirlcle filled with a huge bird, his arms (or
wings, I guess) crossed, tough and bright-eyed. The

sign reads, *El Gallo Mas Gallo!* This bird, his wings crossed and muscular in the red bullseye of that logo, his huge red beak and coxcomb combed back like a 50s greaser, both amuses and bothers me. I have seen him all across the country and for the longest time I haven't been quite able get it—my Spanish is not quite good enough. Literally it means, *the rooster most rooster* or *the most rooster-ish of all the roosters*. Which made no sense. As I ride past this bullseyed rooster this morning something clicks in my head and I get it. Suddenly it makes sense. *The biggest cock on the block.* That's what the logo means. And here's the weirder thing. That rooster? He looks just like my friend Dave who waits beyond the the coastal mountains somehere, waits at the beach, up one more long climb.

Dave is a big man with a bigger moustache, thick chested with a love of life that meet his frame in a powerful laugh. He is the owner of the café—a small sandwhich shop, really—where I work in Colorado, at the base of the ski lodge, where right now, in this late April, the world has turned to mud and no one is visiting. I worked the whole season managing the place and trying to keep our collection of stoned employees shuffling in and out of task, and skiing day after day. I skied a hundred days over the season until the snow turned to slush and then to mud and the mountains were a tiresome slog. We both wanted out, wanted light and green and sun and sand and something else. Dave said Costa Rica. I said bikes. And we went.

I slip the bike into a lower gear and spin out of town, down the road to a green sign that reads Dominical and points in two opposite directions. Neither looks like the road that should climb over the mountains that I find on my map. One direction points to a clear dead-end in a labyrinthian tire yard (chain-link and rust, the racks of black wheels stacked in a maze), the other back to town, past the small church with its lumpy steeple like a bell set down atop a stack of stones. Both say Dominical. A third road (the only one without a sign) leads up into the hills, snaking across up and out of sight into the green and gold of April in Costa Rica, up toward the sky.

I have been in Costa Rica for a while now, and I know the Tico's skill with road signs lacks a certain something, so I choose the road without a sign. I choose the road that goes up, the road less traveled that climbs. Because that's what I do. I climb. Aching and sore, bone weary from yesterday's ride, I climb and climb again with the sun turning the soft, gauzy mist of a tropical morning into a blaze of green. The road churns up corner after corner, through cuts sliced into the red hillsides, and I follow each bend in the road that hides the next. I climb, and again the slow rhythm of ascent builds in me, a thousand meters over a few hours, up and swerving around switchbacks, climbing through the reek of bus exhaust that smells strangely of french toast, climbing with the sun and the mounting heat, and then to the top where the Pacific will appear (I desperately hope) in a wide sweep of blue-gone-white fading into a sky bothered with clouds. This climb is nothing compared to yesterday's but I am dead against the load of my bike, my legs soggy and heavy as waterlogged wood. I climb and climb. I am a sack of rocks on a bike of lead. I want nothing of this idiocy any more. *I'm almost done.* That becomes my line, my mantra, my meditation, as I crawl around another switchback and up the unending road, tires and garbage in the culverts of the small streams. *I'm almost done.* My pounding breath, my thudding heart. *I'm almost done.* Standing now, my legs jamming the pedals to the road. Red mud and a trickle of water in the culverts beside the road. *I'm almost done.* A sad and pathetic version of the little engine that could.

Then I see the top. The road vanishes over the final swale of green and asphalt, where a tiny restaurant, *Miravista*, appears notched into the roadside at the peak. One final climb, one climb and then the descent. One last stretch of asphalt points like a launch ramp up into the sky. Beyond it lies the ocean. That ocean that builds the clouds that come in afternoons and dump their buckets against the mountains. That warm ocean of ease and peace. The sun is at my back as I crest the hill and slide down the windward side of the range, catching the scent of the sea and the chatter of sulpher-winged parakeets as they chitter overhead in fat flocks. The wind flows against me, up from the beach into the hills and mountains, but the descent is sweet. I drop toward that wide swath of sand and sun and cloud, beaches running north and south as far as my eyes can manage, cut only by the estuaries of heavy rivers carrying their loads of water back down from the mountains.

I coast into Dominical by lunch. And by Dominical, I mean a T in the road where the mountain highway meets the sea and can go no further. By Dominical I mean a collection of shacks along a long, coconut-strewn beach and the tall *palapa* of a crossroads restaurant. Stoners and surfers. Ex-pats and Ticos. I feel right at home. This smear of sand the color of olives where the surf pounds and the sun and sky gather. Empty. Just me and my bike as I pull in and drag the wheels through the sand to dunk my head in the ocean that tastes of salt and sun and fish and relief. Dripping and grinning, I pull my bike back across the sand and into the shade of the lone restaurant. The tall *palapa* open to the air and the road and the dust of the day, a space welcome as sleep after a long day. The thatched roof and the wooden tables. The smell of *gallo pinto* and *pantacones*, rice and beans and fried plantains.

I order ceviche and beer. I order coffee—rich and dark as the volcanic dirt of the hillsides above me. I order *el plato del dia*; whatever they've got, I'll eat it. Then, suddenly, scampering around the jigsaw of old chairs, there's a howler monkey. I have seen and heard howlers—*mono congo*—across the contry, but always in the distant trees. Their booming calls echo through the forest like groans. I have never seen one this close. It scampers into the dining room from somewhere. Small and deep chestnut—almost black—with a thick ruff of fur around her shoulders. A female, I guess, since she's petite and feminine and doesn't have the thick-shouldered, gargoyle-menace of the males. She shuffles over to me, at my feet, and looks up with dark eyes full of meaning, like a dog's. She purses her lips. She stares at me for what feels like a long time, small black face and skin like patent leather. Her nose twitching. I lower my hand and she takes it, like a handshake but not quite; more like a courtier kissing the hand of the king. She puts her face to my hand. Instead of a kiss, she smells me, again the way a dog might, quick, repeated sniffs to guage my character, and then looks back at my face. When I don't pull away she clambers—hand over hand—up my arm, her grip strong, immensely strong, and perches on my shoulder.

I stay still. She stays still. I pull my head back to look at her but she's too close, her face too large. It's like looking at a lover. That face dark and blurry with proximity. I can feel her on my shoulder. I can see her bulk from the corner of my eye. She starts pulling and teasing my wet hair, my long wet hair, like straw matted with damp sand. She's combing it with her fingers, the dried leather of them, and I swear she pulls an insect from my hair and quickly eats it.

The waitress brings my ceviche and my beer. The small plate of cold fish cooked in lime juice and cilantro, garnished with a sleeve of saltine crackers. The beer golden and beading the glass with water already. The monkey leaps from my shoulders and scampers.

"¿De dónde es el mono?" Where's that monkey from? My Spanish is formal and schoolboy-ish.

"Su madre fue asesinada. Ella era bebé, así que la llevamos. A la gente le gusta..." She shrugs and walks back to the kitchen. It takes me a while to unravel the Spanish. I get the first sentence, sort of. Her mother was assassinated? Oh, killed, I say in my head. Killed. I get it. When she was a baby her mother was killed and they took her in. Not really legal, I know, but so what? There are four species of monkey in Costa Rica—spider monkeys, squirrel monkeys, white-faced capuchins, and then howlers—and all of them are endangered.

Mainly from habitat loss and hunting, which is probably what happened to her mom. Some people still hunt monkeys for bush-meat, for subsistence. Killing the mom was probably easy. Howlers come down pretty low sometimes. A quick shot into the trees and she falls, but then, there on the ground with her, clinging to her, a baby. Big eyes and skinny arms, her black fur still thin, showing her shockingly gray skin. What do you do? Confronted with all the triggers that evoke pity in us, the wimpering infant, the big head and small, fragile body, huge eyes welling with an almost incomprehensible loss and confusion, that sense of animal connection wins out, and you take her home with you. Sure, it's illegal—endangered species cannot be hand-raised, cannot be traded or sold—but who's going to say anything? And now she's used to people and can never go back, never be released back into the rainforest. Now she's going to spend her fragile life here in this little shack of a restaurant by the sea. There are worse fates.

I look up from my food, already on my second beer and then, suddenly, there he is, Dave. *El gallo mas gallo*. The most rooster of all. He steps from his car and walks into the shade of the hacienda. Chest huge and arms swinging. There's no way it should be this easy to find each other again. We said Dominical, but neither of us had ever been here. We said Dominical, but it was just a spot on the map then. We said Domincal. I guess we just hoped it would turn out all right. It did.

I stand to meet him and clack my way across the cement pad on my bike cleats. I embrace him like I am Cortés and he is the King of Spain.

"Jesus, look at you. You look like shit," he says.

"Good to see you, too." I shake my still soggy hair, long and dirty now and teased by the howler. The wet mop of it has sopped my shoulders and back and hangs into my face. He grimaces. I am sweaty and grimy from two days on the road. My hands are black with grease from my chain, from the multiple times I had to re-mesh it with the gears after downshifting too

32

fast, trying to pull the last bit of momentum out of my climb. I walk like a cowboy whose legs are bowed out from years ahorse.

"It's only been two days." He looks appalled.

"They were rough days."

"I guess so. What happened?"

So we sit and I tell Dave my story, this story that I will tell everyone who will listen for the next few years, as the howler clambers around us, and on us, up the backs of the chairs and across our shoulders like a toddler. I tell him the story of where I hallucinated. Where I wept. The story where I went up and up and never stopped. The story of the time I almost died.

"You have a lot of these stories," he says.

"Reports of my death have been greatly exaggerated."

"Yeah, by you."

I laugh and order another beer. I am done. Dave is here. I can put my bike away and never climb again. I can put my bike away and finish this story, this story about the time I almost died, but that story never ends. It starts again now, like this: we eat and pack the gloriously clean car trunk with my bike, sand spilling off the wheels, and get in. Rolling down his window, he leans out into the road dust to check traffic and turns north onto the Costanera Sur, the coastal highway, toward Manuel Antonio. The hot air flows in and smells of frangipani and diesel. The road leaves the beach and we move through farmland, low fields of rice like waterlogged grassland, spindly papaya trees heavy with thick fruit, and pineapple farms, rows and rows of the huge, dusty-jade, aloe-esque plants topped with the balled spike of the fruit.

"I always thought pineapples grew on trees," says Jim.

"So did I. What the hell?"

Wide scarves of black, fabric-tented greenery mark *viveros*—plant nurseries—where in the shade, ornamental plants are grown for export. Long rows of trees become teak plantations. Even grander are the acres of palm-oil palm. Thick, meaty trees with crosshatched-bark and broad interlocking canopies. They look like unending Greek columns fading off into the distance, each tree's plinth decorated with the clusters of hanging nuts like giant bundles of grapes. We drive for miles through the temples of these farms.

The road turns to dirt, turns to a rutted mess of puddles and dust. It wanders through villages, flat and hot beneath the pounding sun and coated with road dust. The pastel buildings sit in a washed out hum of pink and teal and yellow, along river banks or beside soccer fields and small churches. They are all topped with corrugated red roofing, long faded to a soft orange by the powerful sun. We cross a bridge over a shallow river—a dilapidated, rattletrap bridge of old steel and fresh lumber. Planking laid out across the girders. Above the gaps. Big gaps.

I stiffen in my seat.

"No worries. I came this way this morning," Dave says. He smiles his rooster smile.

I am not so sure. The bridge looks like something I made on the floor as a child with my ERECTOR Set, with those flat wands of tin, flimsy and small. Nothing that will hold the weight of the car. Dave eases the car out onto the witchery of the bridge, the wire and steel held together with a magic of hope and faith and a casual understanding of engineering. The car bumps and jostles across the loose, broken mesh, climbs onto the thick boards that cross the gaps. The planks bang on the metal. The sunlight pounds down. We make it across.

We cross more bridges like the first. Each just as rickety and banging as we purr in our car over the narrow gullies churning with water turned clay-colored and muddy with runoff. There are occasional signs that read ¡Peligro Cocodrilos! and I crane my head as we cross each shallow, bouldered river, the heavy mud of the banks red as Georgia clay. Rio Savegre. Rio Naranjo. The water muddy as milked coffee. Volcanic stones in the current frothing the water to foam. No crocodiles.

We make it to Manuel Antonio by late afternoon, a small National Park that flows around a sequence of scalloped coves between two headlands—Punta Quepos and Punta Cathedral—and find a cheap hotel down along the beach. Just two small beds and a hanging light like something left over from an interrogation. A stream of ants crawls along one wall. Not a thin line, mind you, but a three-foot wide black stream of ants crossing the whole damn room, dividing the wall in half. They appear from a crack in the plaster and surge across the room and down into the corner where they disappear. But there is no time for them. The sun is setting. Fast. Like nothing I have ever seen. It drops in a blaze through the last line of the horizon's clouds—so quickly I can actually see it descend through the sky—toward the thin slice of sea visible between headlands. We walk down to the beach in the warm rush of fresh air, the light golden then amber then auburn. The sun muscles through the clouds, spears out its last rafters against the ceiling of the sky, and winks out. The whole thing lasts five minutes. It happens so fast I can almost feel the earth spinning away from the sun, the surging whirl of the ground beneath my feet as it pulls towards the east.

§

Siddhartha Gautama, in one of his past lives, the ones he revisits sitting beneath the Bodhi tree for 49 days of concentrated meditation as he battles with illusion, in this one life he walks into the forest and finds a starving tigress, her cubs—starving equally—mewling around her in piles. He knows that if she dies they will all die, but to live she will need to kill and eat her own cubs. He thinks that this is the very face of suffering; this animal is not what suffering *resembles* but what it *is*. So, to honor her, to honor it (*suffering*, that is, the reality of it, as opposed to the illusion), he lays himself down before the tigress and allows himself to be eaten.

§

I wake in the morning like a new man, reborn after a few beers and a long, long sleep. The ants are gone. Whatever mysterious errand they were after, I am guessing they have arrived and dismantled it.

In Manuel Antonio the beach is clean and quiet. Empty this late morning. Just off the point, a series of small rock outcrops and islands jut from the ragged ocean, supporting nesting colonies of brown boobies, terns, and magnificent frigate birds that cut up the air like flying knives. We cross into the park, fording the shallow estuary at the end of the public beach and find the entrance closed—*Cerrado los Lunes* reads the sign hanging across the trail. Closed Mondays. Oh well. There is nothing to do but swim in the ocean and lay on the beach. *Nothing to do. Nothing to do.* I like this mantra better. We head back to the beach.

The day pours down on us, the waves slamming on the flat sand. Pelicans scour the coastline with their javelin bodies, running inches above the water in front of the crashing waves. I plop down in the sand. We spend the morning bodysurfing and lounging like seals on the nearly empty beach—I guess there is something to say for coming to the park when it's closed. By late in the day the sun still pounds and I am famished—empty the way you get when you spend hours in the water—and we are red and roasted and burned from the wind.

We trudge up the beach to where a rough, painted wooden sign hangs nailed to a tree in a grove of coconut palms—*Mar y Sombra*. Sea and Shade. Indeed. The shade feels deep and wet as we enter the restaurant from the heavy sun, like a dive into cold water. We land at a table of old boards, weather-beaten and gray, across a pair of sawhorses.

"*Dos aguas y dos margaritas*," we say to the woman who slides out from behind the bar. Her small white hat, like a 50s soda jerk's, her amused smile at the two of us. Dave, towering like that rooster even in his chair, and me, thin and shaggy with a burned face, rough with a days-old beard and a wet coil of woven bracelets up my left arm. The low shack of the place fits perfectly among the towering trees. The castaway feel, the oasis of the place—it is perfect. Small spatters of sunlight make it through the palm fronds. Bob Marley's "Three Little Birds" bubbles from a speaker behind the bar and ice chinks in the glasses she brings. After slugging back the cold, cold water—slaking the heavy thirst of ocean and wind—the margaritas taste first of salt and then of sugar and sour and orange. Made fresh with the juice of the *mandarina*, a sour orange used all over the country, they taste like the ripe fruit of sunlight chilled in a glass.

We order burgers and *patacones* and more drinks, the world comfortable and at home around us. The thatched hut beneath the tall columns of palms, wind sneaking in through the grove to cool us, wind carried so far from where it begins in the wild, blue emptiness out beyond the horizon. The world feels made for us, right and ordered and comfortable. It feels like home. But then it starts. Slowly at first; a small, sudden jerking at my feet. A shaking that jumps to our table, the beer frothing in our glasses, and then my chest and then the trees and then the sky and the wind and then everything is liquid, everything is fluid and flown. Everything leaps. The castaway metal roof covering part of the patio bangs and clatters. The air roars like a train or a tornado—that sound, it comes from everywhere—and dishes crash in the hidden kitchen. The woman with her white hat appears in the doorway, her eyes wide with fear. She braces herself against the frame of the door. I get it, suddenly— earthquake. She's doing what we are supposed to, what we are too clueless and stunned to try: find cover.

Instead, we sit there, Dave and I, dumb as stumps, as the world turns to froth. The table bounces; the plates and drinks dance into the sand. My body bobbles and hops in the chair, like I am young again and dandled on my father's knees, that weird staccato jiggle. I try and stand and stumble like a drunk, the world wild below me. The sand buzzes beneath my feet and the roar goes on and on. Like an airplane turbine, like a thousand vacuums, like an immense congregation of lions. The palm trees bend back and forth like the wild swaying of forty metronomes all keeping different time. Their fronds snap like flags in the wind. They bend and jitter and my vision seems wrong. Everything is buzzing. The world beyond the restaurant is a blur, made fuzzy by motion. The sky could fall in and it wouldn't surprise me.

"Shit! Dave yells.

"Holy shit!" I yell.

"*¡Dios ayúdeme!*" The woman yells.

I look out to sea and the horizon is dancing, or my eyes are wobbling or the earth is. Nothing makes sense. Nothing is right anymore. There is nothing solid left in the world. Everything is trying to get somewhere else only to be stopped by everything else trying to get there too. The world howls. The sand keeps shoving itself into the sea and the sea into the sand. The trees reach for something they can't quite touch. It goes on and on, this shaking, this rattling. The buzz in the air, this weird everywhere-roar, ricochets from tree to tree. The roof bangs. The sand froths.

Then it slows—the shaking sand, the trees ticking down to steadiness like a countdown. A countdown to stability that is only an illusion, now that I know what the world is capable of, like treachery from a dear friend, like betrayal. The world shouldn't do this, I think. The world shouldn't, but it just did. The sand stops its jittering and quiets down. I release the table I didn't know I was gripping.

"*Que grande,*" the woman says, crossing herself. "*Un macho.*"

No shit, I think. *Now that was the real* gallo mas gallo.

§

This earthquake, I would learn in later days, was centered off the southern Caribbean coast, near a river mouth and estuary of islands called *Bocas del Toro*, the mouth of the bull. 47 people lost their lives, mostly in Puerto Viejo where we had been just three days ago, where roads were lifted and shifted more than 12 feet in some places and then the ocean returned in huge waves, brown with froth and wreckage. Measuring 7.6 on the Richter scale, the quake was the strongest in the recorded history of the country, a country that has a lot of earthquakes, it should be said. The *Bocas del Toro* quake lifted the Caribbean coast and destroyed houses across the country. It shut down the banana railroad that had run from Limon to San José for more than one hundred years—shut it down permanently—when all its bridges collapsed and the tracks shifted into sudden S-curves. We were more than 100 miles away on the beach in Manuel Antonio and still it felt like death arriving on a shaking horse.

Below us here in Costa Rica, the buoyant Coco plate slams into the Caribbean plate and dives beneath it in a subduction zone, driving mountains into the sky and lava to the surface in a chain of volcanoes that runs along that cordillera. The two plates resist each other, of course. They jar up against one another like rival males facing off. At 15:57 local time, the earth slipped; the Coco plate jerked down deeper and shoved the Caribbean almost 1.5 meters (5 feet!) into the air. Roads were shredded and railway tracks uprooted. Houses collapsed and reassembled themselves in piles of wreckage. Tsunamis rushed into Puerto Viejo, 10 feet high in places, and filled that flat city with water. In Manuel Antonio, a huge landslide dropped thousands of tons of wreckage and stone onto *Playa Escondido*, the hidden beach where we had hoped to hike to that day. There are so many ways to die—and we missed them all. We watched from a bar on the beach, drinks in our hands shining like luck, as the world shook itself the way a wet dog does and then settled back to normal.

§

The woman moves quickly, begins cleaning up the glasses fallen behind the bar. I look and Dave is already righting the fallen chairs, organizing the dining area. The café owner in him taking charge of the chaos. *El gallo mas gallo.* He tilts our table and slops the water and ice and tequila into the sand. He stoops to collect our food and fills the trash with it. I stand shaking—as if all the earth's movement had just been given to me. I can't move and I am moving. I buzz and hum like a huge bee. The world's fluidity has found my legs and my balls, and it sits there purring like a pet cat. My stomach roils and turns. I feel like puking.

Soon the place is working again and the woman with her small, wide face brings us new burgers, brings us new drinks, as if nothing had happened. She smiles almost apologetically beneath her tiny white hat, her skin the color of the sand that now lies so peacefully out there under the sun, stroked by the waves' continuous attention. She smiles and lets out a deep sigh, looking me right in the face, blowing a small wisp of hair from her eyes, and I let out a deep sigh too. One that I didn't know I was holding. I look out to sea and the pelicans are there, coasting across the unchanged waters. And further out, diving into the deepest blue for fish.

III.

These are the stories I tell my students who are headed to Costa Rica for my environmental-writing course ten years after. By now I have left Colorado and gone to grad school to study nature writing and poetry, of all things. And I have found a job at a small college where they are letting me take a group of students south this January, to explore ideas of place and how we tell our stories. So to start off, I tell the students my stories. I want them to be ready for the Costa Rica they are about to enter, the one I remember. A world that followed its own rules and felt unruffled by the average, unexpected power failure or earthquake. But this year, ten years after that first adventure into the clouds, after the world turned liquid beneath my feet, it's me who isn't ready. The airport in San José is finished and new—more like Orlando or Atlanta than the Third World puzzle I remember. We never touch the tarmac and the quonset-hut feeling is gone, replaced with clean, well-lighted space. I am disappointed. The students seem at ease and at home, even as they fidget and wonder aloud about immigration and customs. After we're through—the customs agent doesn't look twice at our bags, or us for that matter—there's the usual thatch of people waiting beyond smoked windows. Pressed against the glass their faces look like a Munch street scene—the distorted *anomie* of all that's modern. We gather beyond the customs kiosks as I count heads. The crowd beyond the window is still watching. The students feel like they are on display.

The taxi drivers are aggressive; they bark and badger, but our guide is there with a sign and we are quickly hustled through to the waiting van. The van is clean and comfortable; the guide's English, tinged with a Caribbean patois, is excellent. The doors close with a hiss and we are off.

That was too easy, I think, as I sit, vaguely listening to the guide explaining the itinerary. *How are they going to learn anything?*

§

On this long swale of beach, the Corcovado Peninsula jutting out from the southwest corner of Costa Rica, where the land rises up green and primordial from the sea, brown pelicans ride the surf with no purpose I can find beyond beauty. On an olive-colored beach at the edge of one of the largest untrammeled patches of rainforest left in Central America, this wild shelf of green land where the air churns with macaws and the cries of howler monkeys and the whole day resembles the world at first light, the perfection of an eternal dawn, these birds drop down in tight lines as waves pile into the shore. Their bodies look carved, so solid are they in the air. Like scalpels, like scythes. They move easily through the power of the wind that comes a long way across the Pacific, through the faultless clarity of the sunlight and the fresh surf. The birds ride the waves like surfers, the tips of their enormous wings almost touching the water; they ride the swell of air, each wave pushing as it draws water up from the trough into a crashing curl. The pelicans ride each wave until the last possible moment when it breaks in a wash of white foam. At the zero point, the birds kick out and rise subtly off the edge of the wave with a few fast pumps of their wings, then, in tight formation, beak to tail, and with something close to perfection, they drop in again.

§

Costa Rica has changed in the ten years since my first visit. It has carefully groomed itself and the face it presents to new visitors is modern and clean. Tourism, especially ecotourism, is one of the nation's most productive industries now and it shows. The roads around San José are wide and neat. Hotel chains have grown up like mushrooms—Hampton, Comfort, and Holiday Inns. Casinos light up the roads like used car dealerships. The girls (the 15 students in my class are all women; I teach at a women's college) are excited and chatty. Our guide, Luis, is short and strong with a wide forehead and a wider smile. He has a line of gold piercings running up the whole of his left ear and speaks with a soft Caribbean tinge. He asks some of the girls' names and changes them to their Spanish equivalents. *Adriana, Maria Catherina, Mo.* He doesn't quite know what to do with Mo. They get him to pronounce Pittsburgh, which comes out like *Pissburgh*. They laugh. He laughs. He asks them to roll an R. The bus fills with a buzz like a hive of bees.

§

Pelicans are big-winged birds, strong gliders that have little need for the extra shove of air that the waves provide. I have seen them in flocks a hundred strong high in the air, coasting the vertiginous shore in strict regiments. "Costa Rica's Air Force" the local joke goes, since the country abolished its military in 1949. Their surfing acrobatics are also risky—too close, and a wave might snap across a wing, tumbling the bird into the surf, possibly to drown. They are not fishing along the waves, either. Pelicans fish from high above, circling until they spot their prey loitering near the surface. Tucking their wings in like peregrine falcons, they arrow down and hit the water hard, surfacing with a pouch fat and wriggling with fish. When they move across the surf in squadrons of precision, the awkward waddling gait they use on land is gone, replaced by a kind of aeronautical perfection. They are grace and purpose in the air, the shuttle crossing the weave of the surf. I watch them for hours some mornings and can't find a reason for their actions beyond pure delight in their ability. But maybe I just don't know enough.

§

The next morning, Luis and I gather the students in the van and drive up and out of San José and into the *Cordillera Central*, between the hidden summits of the Irazú and Barva volcanoes. Coffee plantations, neat as weaving on the sides of the foothills, give way to a riot of huge leaves—leather banana and poor man's umbrella—as we pass through *Braulio Carrillo National Park*. Long, tendriled lianas and the silver-edged leaves of the winter's bark trees. Clouds and banners of mist. Wild impatiens dot the roadside with red and purple. The confetti of wild kings.

I am sitting up front with Mo and Adrienne, two sophomores who couldn't be more different if they tried. Mo—short for Maureen—is tall and thin and boyish by choice, with a kind of laconic cool. She doesn't appear to take anything seriously, but I can tell she is listening. Adrienne is small and dark with a hawk's nose, short hair, and a sharp wit. She is always willing to challenge me.

We dive into a deep tunnel through the misted hillsides that climb up like walls on either side of the road. Darkness lit only by the trailing streamers of the taillights of the cars ahead. The tunnel is long and deep, damp with water that seeps through the ceiling like tears. We travel in silence, the girls and I in the dark; even Luis is quiet now, and then suddenly we break into the open air again, the powerful green of the hillsides falling away into the air, into the clouds and distance. We have crossed the divide, that suddenly. Moved from one watershed to another and are on the other side of the continent among mountains and rivers that now fall away toward the Caribbean like the fingers of an open hand. We descend into the emerald palm of this new world.

Further down, as we cross the huge span of bridge that arches across the *Río Sucio*, two huge streams come together beneath us in a broad wash of stone spangled with tufts of alder and low willows. One river, sulfur-yellow and thick, looks like flowing mud; the other is crystal, the blue-white of glacier milk. The crystalline blue of *Río Honduras* flows out from the uncut rainforest above. It looks right and proper and tropical. It looks healthy. It looks like nature. *Río Sucio*, the dirty river, on the other hand, looks sick. Its water is the color of old egg yolks and smears of rust mark the stones along its banks. It looks like a river that has spent too much time among humans. Sick, polluted, wrong.

"God, what's up with that water?" Adrienne asks. Her voice carries just a twinge of valley-girl pique.

"Nothing," Luis smiles his huge smile. He expected the question, clearly. "Nothing. That guy

comes from springs below from *Volcán Irazú*. Up there."
He's pointing up the valley into the green and mist of the *Braulio Carrillo* and beyond into the clouds. "You can't see it now. The water carries iron and sulfur deposits down from volcano. Makes the water this color. Is good. There are fish in there."

"Whoa. Really?"

"Good for farmers, that water. "

Below the bridge the two rivers join and mix in a violent churn, parallel for a short stretch—mustard against sapphire—before they blend to a copper green topped with white where the water bangs against boulders dragged years ago out of the mountains. The rivers blend for a short stretch until the weight of the dirty water takes over, the smaller *Honduras* finally subsumed in the swath of iron and sulfur and mud. A dark ochre smear burned into the landscape. Beautiful it ain't.

I am worried about beauty because I am trying to find some way of talking to my students—and to myself, if I am honest—about the attraction the natural world has for us (for me). Why is nature so often defined by beauty and why do we respond to and feel healed in nature? Why do we feel some sort of connection to something so much larger than ourselves? These seem like easy questions, but like most easy questions, once you dive into them, things get messy. On the rough edge of the world, across this bridge over two rivers, I am working out one of the dominant tropes in Western philosophy and poetry. I hope my students appreciate it.

My mind finds beauty in the world—in those pelicans back in Corcovado, for example—because, as one argument goes, it sees the echo of the divine in a fragmented and downtrodden world; in nature, the human soul finds a resonance in the work of its creator. So the pelicans' tangent across the water is beautiful not because it holds some kind of intrinsic value, but because the tight flight of those huge birds inches above thudding and curling waves echoes some kind of avian grace that exists external to these birds, in the mind or in the spirit. This is classic Platonic thought that becomes Neo-Platonic when it collides with Christianity. Like Plato says, *beholding beauty with the eye of the mind, he will be enabled to bring forth, not images of beauty, but realities.* The specific image of the pelican—in the word, in the world, or in the eye—is a flawed copy that calls the observer or the writer back to that perfect reality that exists in the elsewhere.

So now when I try and describe this world, or worse, when I try to get college students to articulate it, our images feel flaccid. Weak tea compared to the strong Costa Rican coffee that surrounds us. I can offer up the names of plants—wild ginger's magenta torches or the green leather of the sea grape's leaves—beside me or in memory. I can talk about the dun and ochre of the pelicans churning across the waves. I can explain how two rivers seam together in a field of fluid stone. I can try to evoke the sun as it descends though the ardent blue of the sky in its rapid arc of fire to a welcoming sea. But what have I accomplished? What more do I know about nature for having said these things?

This is partially the point, isn't it, for Plato? Plato's problem with poetic images of natural beauty seems to be that they are easy to love but do no real labor. They are the toddlers of philosophy. They ratchet up an immediate emotional agenda in the mind. They bang on the floor and demand to be acknowledged. They sob and moan and knock like windows in a big wind, they drip like rain from an overflowing roof. They carry flowers in hands grubby with creosote and swim miles through the sea uttering their windy, nearly human songs. But they are not real. That's the other half of his argument. Only beauty seen in the mind, in the recesses of the rational self, is real: *not images of beauty, but realities*, in other words. The physical world and the words we use to describe it— both of them!—are mere copies, to Plato's mind, of that larger purity of form that floats in the ether of the logical.

"Seriously, Jeff," says Adrienne. "What the hell are you talking about?"

§

Dropping out of the mountains and the cloud forest, we float down into the flat, Caribbean lowlands. We watch ecosystems change by the kilometer as we lose elevation, down to the coastal plain, down into the Del Monte banana plantations. For kilometers we are surrounded: banana trees twenty feet high on either side, thick and concentrated. We're riding through a tropical tunnel. Thick ditches dug in the earth and narrow conveyor belts with dangling hooks slice between the trees with leaves huge and rubbery. The company houses that fill in the gaps between plantations are small, pastel and poor, laid out in grids with a church and a soccer field for every tiny town. Dirt floors and chickens. Small gardens on the southern side draped with banana fronds.

We are headed for *Parque Nacional Tortuguero* on the Caribbean coast—a wide, swampy estuary draining most of the northern Caribbean slope. Accessible only by boat or by plane, the park is home to three of four species of monkey native to Costa Rica, both species of toucan, lizards, caiman, crocodiles, sharks, and innumerable herons, ospreys, and egrets. There are jaguars, ocelots, and jaguarundis, though all are rarely seen. Guides have gone years, Luis says, working daily trips through the park, without catching site of even one, only to be stunned, one day, as a mother and her two cubs swim *Río Tortuguero*, their heads up in the dark swirl of the water and their legs pumping, and cross to the barrier islands to hunt the park's namesake turtles.

There are strangler figs that arrive as shit in the rainforest canopy when a groove-billed ani, perhaps, spatters the bark of an almond with its salt-and-pepper, plaster-textured shit. The seeds of the fig tree kick out aerial roots and live at first on sunlight and dust alone, drinking the afternoon rain. Thin as skin the roots drop from the tree branches, dropping meters and meters before finally reaching the earth. Grimed with moss by the time they hit the floor (where they become heavy and woody and curled like double-helixed monkey ladders), the roots thicken and then ring the host tree with their mass; they shutter the host almond tree in buttresses of arch and wing. The fig strangles the rotted parent and it dies and decays, but the fig, held aloft by the wings of its hardened roots, keeps standing, hollow now as a pipe.

At *Caño Blanco*, the students and I board flat-bottom boats and slip quickly into the back end of this canal system. *Tortuguero* is huge, swampy and flat. The rivers that feed it—the *Chirripo, Suerte, Sierpe,* and others—crisscross into a remarkable network of canals and waterways. Some are the color of molasses, deep tannin black, some *café con leche*. Some are slow, imperceptibly pushing towards the Caribbean. Others are stronger, more aggressive, more obviously rivers. We follow the main channel north, through thick bands of raffia and coconut palm. Little blue herons lift up and sweep their wings into the air as we pass. An osprey tears into a fish carcass on the muddy bank. Anhingas pose stoically on old snags, their wings spread to dry, the males with their golden heads arrowed up towards the sky. Sleek and elegant swimmers who spear fish, snakes, and even small caiman with their sharp, hooked bills, anhingas, like cormorants, don't produce any oil. Their feathers, then, become totally saturated when they dive, helping them move through the water as they hunt. It takes them time to dry out. Especially here, where more than 5 meters of rainfall a year is a regular occurrence.

The students only show passing interest in the birds. Maybe we are moving too fast. Maybe it's all too new. Maybe they are just birds and the students were hoping for more, hoping to see that image of the rainforest they carry in their minds, the whole live ocelot of the rainforest in one perfect moment. They are mostly silent, snapping an occasional picture as the trees and clouds rush past. Egrets flash brilliant white against the deep green canvas of the palms when the sun paints them. The rainforest presses in against the riverbanks and threatens like storm clouds. We stop for lunch—fresh fruit, pineapple like ambrosia, pita, and cookies—and then Luis finds something that hooks them. A golden silk spider. Huge. Easily the size of a child's open hand with a rectangular body and long, elegant legs striped iridescent green and spotted gold. The female spins a strong golden web with silk that the native tribes once gathered and used for fishing line. The girls crowd around and laugh as Mo strums the threads of the web like guitar strings. They are strong and not at all sticky.

"See that smaller spider sharing the web with her? Is her mate," Luis says. She is easily twenty times his size.

"Really? Cool," Mo says and there is a general murmur of agreement. This fact resonates; it validates their unspoken belief that nature is maternal. They have found a way in. A piece of the world to think about and understand.

We encounter pieces and fragments of the world, and never the totality. That much Plato and I can agree on. But I am unwilling or unable to call these fragments broken or damaged. That spider appears perfectly at home in its octagonal web inside the canopy of a small breadfruit tree. The pelican, even awkward and gawky as it can be, appears remarkably tuned to its landscape as it slices through the air, blasted off the face of the waves. It is a well-made tool. But there it is; I have done it again. Both "well-made" and "tool" imply a toolmaker, a shaper who exists in the otherwhere. It's hard to talk about grace and beauty without pointing toward something outside the world. The structure of our language—the way words abstract experience from the world where that experience happens—isolates us from nature and that very isolation often means we look for something beyond the world to complete the world. In the very metaphors we use, our language regularly suggests a distance from the world, a kind of brokenness and isolation that Plato laments, and that I, finally, want to celebrate. It is true, I think, that at some level they represent oppositional constructions—the world outside our minds and the world of words our minds creates—but like most oppositions, such juxtaposition is a well-crafted and necessary fiction.

They are the two most complicated entities that we encounter on a daily basis: language and the natural world. Each is intricate, almost beyond comprehension, and yet each presents itself to us in chunks of articulation that allow us to believe in our ability to grasp and command these forces. Language almost means. It comes close and then at the final moment veers away. Pelican, we say. Fig tree. River and egret. The fire of the sun as it relaxes into the sea. The road up to *Cerro de la Muerte* disappearing into cloud. Our words are an archive of our limited experience in that most physical of worlds; we could not have a language devoid of context. But we only understand those pieces of the world that we have named and our understanding is limited and fragmentary. Like Adam in one of our original stories, we live in a language and a landscape of our own naming, but—like Adam again, during that long first morning in the garden with the world shining around him fresh and watered with its immaculate newness—we stumble, somewhat baffled, through this world we have named despite our potential for power and control.

Our immediate experience in the world is visceral and concrete—it is never abstract; that's essential. Our world is rich and overflowing with itself, almost violently so, but our understanding of this world and our status within it is dependent upon the interaction of, and the tension between, the natural world and the world of words. We (I) cannot say anything fully and with finality. We (I) do not possess that kind of power. This is just as Plato argues, concerning the immortality of the soul: *To describe it as it is would require a long exposition of which only a god is capable; but it is within the power of man to say in shorter compass what it* resembles. That's the key here. What it *resembles*. Instead of articulating the incomprehensible vastness of the world perfectly or fully, or finding forms accessible only to the mind and the rational sense, we must try to find ways to relate the world and its essence to what we can comprehend. We don't define the world at all. Instead, we raise momentary islands of stability out of the larger ocean of experience through language, and we bridge these islands together with constructions of rhetoric. Each island, connected to another, comes to symbolize more than its own isolated meaning by juxtaposition and confluence. Not by echoing a deeper essence beyond the world—sorry, Plato; too bad, Socrates—but by moving from one island to the next, we create archipelagos of significance and anchor our narratives about what it means to know and experience a landscape or a place out of the fragments of our experience.

If the stoic, unknowable whole that exists in God or in Plato's abstract space of forms, if it exists at all, recedes forever before us, available (as even Plato admits) to the rational mind alone, then each fragment we perceive carries a piece of a larger unfinished and unfinishable narrative. Each image, each word branches out from the main trunk like the walled buttress roots of that strangler fig that feeds a flock of red-lored parrots along *the Río Tortuguero*, their vibrant wing bars shining like the chevrons of happy soldiers. The wholeness of the tree can be defined alone in the unaccountable accumulation of its parts and the stories it stars in. A wholeness we encounter only in pieces, and in story. In Costa Rican Spanish, for example, the fig tree is *el matapalo*, the tree-killer, and its leaves hang on long petioles, the tincture of which both causes and cures hemorrhage. The fig, too, is Adam and Eve's tree in the Garden of Eden, a source and cover for their shame, and the Bodhi where the Buddha rests in the shade and is surprised by Nirvana in the washed-out sky. The turning ellipticals of its leaves sweep down in a wreckage of his past lives and he must watch and suffer each one again—the son that he abandoned, the wife he left alone in bed. In that story I feel an echo of my own life. Jennifer at home in the city, alone, with our young son. She sits in the window of our small house in Pittsburgh with Julian in her lap, a book before them, and looks out at the flat light of midwinter, the gray-and-brown-and-white of it, the yearly death of it. I have left her there so I might wander and explore and think about trees. Like that sacred tree now covered with oranges and wishes that stands in a corral outside of the holy city of Bodhgaya.

§

In the morning, we leave the small cabins of our lodge, the green metal roofs and dark wood balconies decorated with bright hammocks and tucked into the rainforest, cabins that look out across the thrumming and powerful *Río Tortuguero*. We board the boats again to push up into the park. The main canal is busy with traffic from the town, but we soon leave it behind. Right, left, right, right. We are in a maze-in-reverse, an unknown entrance but an obvious exit. The water is muddy and swirling. Raffia leaves lean out over the water in enormous, distinct fronds. We quickly find a massive, male green iguana perched above the river in the top of a small palm. Five feet long with an orange rooster's crest, large dewlap, and a circular scale spotting his jawline, he looks particularly Cenozoic. He marks his territory for us (or more likely for the smaller, darker female in a nearby tree) by jerking his head up again and again. Below him, Luis spots a small spectacled caiman, maybe 1 meter long, silent and camouflaged in the water lily and hyacinth. The caiman looks like a small crocodile with a short, broad snout and bony eye ridges like the outlines of horn-rimmed eyeglasses. The students push to the front of the boat to try and find it. With a snap of its tail, it splashes out of sight and several of the students gasp and move quickly to the back. That we are twenty times larger than the caiman, that caiman hunt fish and birds, small lizards perhaps, but not humans; none of that matters. It looks dangerous—it is dangerous, and they feel suddenly fragile—and there it is, just off the bow.

Rain begins in a slow spatter that quickly turns heavy. We pull out heavy-duty rain ponchos, blaze yellow, and move upstream like a boatful of convicts: hoods up, heads down. The channel narrows as we move inland, floating among overhanging palms, sea grape, mangroves, and raffia. Fishtail palms, tree ferns, and a variety of heliconias fill in the understory. The heliconia flowers are small cups of nectar—curved and fluted—each particular curve matched with a specific species of hummingbird. The actual flowers are hidden within ladders of colored leaves, flaming red, lemon, and orange, resembling nothing so much as lobster claws. Startling green Jesus Christ lizards (also called basilisks) bask in the overhanging branches of one heliconia. Small, crested lizards the color of jade, they can run across the surface of the water for short stretches. We watch and hope, but no luck. They stay still in their roosts, refusing us this most elemental miracle.

§

Here's another problem, I think as I wait out the rain beneath my hood—the heavy rattle of the water filling up the metal boat. The rainforest, rich and layered and multiple, dense with diversity and life in its manifold possibilities, the over-the-top surprise of a world where behind each leaf lies another, where behind each name rests another—the particular labor of coming to know *this place* parallels the larger struggle to define place in general and create meaning out of our interaction with

54

the world through language. This is why it takes time and patience, something I apparently lack in spades, to access. Nature is a not a door that can simply be walked through, a switch on the wall of the mind that can be flipped to illuminate the perfect beauty of the eternal. The natural world we—me, my students, most of us in the developed world—the world we encounter most often is a tamed and domesticated world, a simplified landscape of garden and plantings pleasant to the eye and occupied by those animals most willing to accommodate themselves to living in our shadow and among our waste, and this domestication furthers our belief that we can understand and make sense of the world in which we live.

We name and define and thus limit and control the world that we experience, I think, but in the tropics there is always another layer, another degree of significance, another story, another danger. The rainforest represents a nearly infinite gradation of meaning and sense, of tree and liana, of species and leaf, of bird and reptile, insect and mammal. We name and we try to know, but each effort only underscores all that is left out. However, if language separates us from the world (and it does, abstract as it is, by definition) it also joins us to the world. Our efforts represent a continuous attempt at control and containment, from which the landscapes of the tropics are constantly slipping.

"Oh God," says Adrienne. "Not this again."

The rain keeps coming, harder and harder. Soon we are all hunched over. Drops slap onto our hoods. The surface of the river is pitted like basalt and the roar of water hitting water is overwhelming. We can't hear a thing. The sky waterfalls down on top of us. A thunder of rain. A stampede. The cocoa-colored river turned to a rough sea beneath the power of the falling sky. Chihiro, my Japanese exchange student, is bent over double and whimpering into her knees. I can hear her say over and over, "I hate the rainforest. I hate the rainforest." Five minutes, ten, we are pelted with what feels like the whole weight of the sea hauled up into the hot clouds and then returned. We are close to turning around when the sun tears a hole in the heavy sky and the rains spatters to a halt.

"A good sign," says Luis. "Everything come out to dry itself off now."

The river smoothes out and high above in the towering canopy, there they are: spider monkeys. They brachiate up in the sun. They move easily hundreds of feet above the ground; their prehensile tails snake out and anchor them on branches that seem far too light to hold their weight. Through the binoculars we make out their chestnut backs and dark facial masks, and watch as the tiny young cling to the stomachs of their mothers. One mother even acts as a bridge for her juvenile who is not quite ready to make the jump between the two trees; she holds on across a gap in the branches with her arms and her tail and the young one scampers between two towering trees across her back.

Just a bit further we round a corner of the dark canal, tall pillars of raffia palm looming up on either side, to find a bare-throated tiger heron warming itself on a sunlit snag. A big bird, as tall as but thicker than a great blue heron, striated gold and black. It stretches out its neck and wings, rolling its small shoulders back so its wings cup and catch the light. It stands there holding that pose, looking reverent, for lack of a better word. The sunlight pours down through the broken clouds and darkens the deep-shadowed forest and the black, reflecting water. The heron glows. It looks Egyptian: the crest of Ra.

§

In the afternoon, the students and I gear up for a hike up *Cerro Tortuguero*—an ancient volcano now worn to a 300-meter nub. Still, it's a dramatic landmark in this flat plain. Red basalt and ancient trees. Spiked waree palm. Ceiba spangled with epiphytes and bromeliads and a few mahogany trees scattered here and there. Most of

Costa Rica's mahogany has been logged for North American furniture markets. Few remain, and even fewer of the size we find here, 50 meters tall and 2 meters in circumference at the base. Mottled bark, green and brown and yellow, smooth to the touch. The soil is shallow and wet so the roots run along the surface for 30 meters and fan out from the trunks in huge buttresses like wings, elegant curtains of living wood.

The rainfall drains off the peak and collects at the base of the volcano, turning the trail to marsh. Often we are knee-deep in a charcoal mud that smells of rot and wet leaves, and we pull our feet free with sucking slurps. The students laugh and splash in the muck; this is the kind of adventure they were hoping for. Among the rotting deadfall along the path, we find the strawberry poison-dart frog. The size of a quarter, it is bright red fading to dark blue-black on its limbs. In Spanish it's *rana con blue jeans*, the blue jeans frog. Plentiful along the Caribbean lowlands, the frogs have few predators and eat mostly ants and mosquitoes. There are several species of poison-dart frogs and the skin secretions were often used on the blowgun darts of indigenous tribes. The poison is a powerful neurotoxin that can cause paralysis and eventually stop breathing.

Howler monkeys move through the canopy above us. They call out in raucous, deep booming calls that echo and fill the forest. These were the calls that woke us early this morning—deep throated gulps of barking sound, terrifying at 4:30 in the morning. I woke from a dream to those bellows with the rain thudding down on the roof—primordial and fierce. Now that we can call them by name, they have much less power over us. Howlers rarely come down to earth, spending most of their time high in the canopy eating leaves. Slow moving, they travel in family groups of ten to twenty and don't brachiate like the spider monkeys we saw this morning. We finally see the howlers through the dense canopy, large shouldered and dark, the heavy male looming protectively over his troupe like a gargoyle.

Back down on the ground, Luis finds a small eyelash viper coiled on the buttressed root of a mahogany. A pungent yellow and camouflaged to look like the flowers and leaves of the heliconia from which it hunts hummingbirds, it is maybe a foot long. Looking closely we can see the horny, spine-like scales above each eye that give it its name. It's a small snake and the students are, really, unimpressed, until Luis says, "That one bite you, in one hour you're dead."

The students back away as one.

The eyelash viper, while dangerous, is not the most poisonous of the snakes in Costa Rica. That honor is shared between the fer-de-lance and the bushmaster. Those two snakes don't mess around. The fer-de-lance's camouflage hides it easily in the leaf-litter scattered across the forest floor, while the bushmaster is a sinister-looking, oiled-black-and-beige javelin with a wedge-shaped head that just looks mean. Both are fortunately rare and, even more fortunately, nocturnal. Still, wildlife biologist Les Belesky reports the story of a man, bitten by a fer-de-lance, whose open wound actually poisoned and killed his wife who was tending him, and bushmasters are rumored to have chased people down and killed them—intentionally. In fact, the name of the bushmaster's genus (*Lachesis*) comes from the Greek and refers to one of the three Fates who determined the length of the thread of life. And in Spanish it is sometimes called *matabuey,* or the ox-killer. Enough said.

§

I'm in the lodge's garden now, the day done, and the sun finishing its trail across the sky is almost hidden in the gathering trees to the west. I have my beer and I am thinking about beauty again, trying to follow its trail in my journal. The garden is beautiful; there is no argument there. The softness of the dusk air, the humidity welcome now as the day cools. Huge orchids and heliconia with long glossy leaves like the banana palm and dangling ladders of orange and red flowers, the color and shape of cooked lobster claws. The slow slide of the river beyond the trees as its gathers together to rush the sea, and lights beginning to come on in the cabins behind me. Beauty and ease. But here's my problem: the heliconia—their flowers dangling like orange rungs in a canopy of leather banana leaves—aren't ladders to the divine. The flight of the pelican is no testament to some elemental perfection. At the same time I understand that the opposite is also hard to fathom. It is difficult to believe that beauty is simply sex and advertisement, simple adaptation to the environment. The scintillated throat of the magnificent hummingbird flashes to catch the eye of a female in the welter of rainforest underbrush—that's true enough—and the pungent yellow of the eyelash viper (so very like the heliconia flowers where it likes to hide) is the ideal camouflage to hunt hummingbirds, but is that all? Is adaptation enough? What about this attraction I feel when confronted with such beauty? Why do I (we) respond to such beauty? And how can the mere description of such life—using only words on the page—give a similar charge?

   If words do anything, then they speak to a fundamental connection between the human mind and the physical world. And systems of language, like systems anywhere, represent structures of sense and naming; they represent constellations of wonder and experience, a joining of the dissimilar, and a radical understanding gathered together in series of sonic-moments. As Emerson says, *All language is fossil poetry.* In other words, at the heart of every utterance once lived a blessed moment of comprehension and meaning, a shining fragment of metaphoric insight that connected mind and world; however, equally inherent in the notion of *fossil* is failure, death, and ossification. These little gems of language—like stones fallen from a sky of infinite possibility, somehow still rich with the remains of lives lived long ago—represent fragments of meaning that define our sense of what can and what cannot be said. We try to speak about the places we live in through image and metaphor—the tools of the poet—because, as Plato says, only a god can say what a thing *is*. The best we can do is to say what it *resembles*. We try to speak about place and the relationship we have with the land, and the words fail. We fail and fail again. Sometimes beautifully.

On the other hand, for Immanuel Kant, beauty presents an intellectual engagement with the world; beauty shows us that the world is ordered and complete. But, for Kant, beauty lies not in the thing itself, but in an act of perception of the thing. Not in the pelican or hummingbird alone, but in communion with my watching eye as the bird arrows down from the deep sky to skim the waves in a wake of joy. The flash of light from the hummingbird's throat that catches in mine, the small sapphire tear streaked back from his eye. Beauty is what we make of what we see in the world; it's what our minds create. Beauty is the frame around the world that permits us to control and corral the abundance of the natural in the act of observation itself—like the Buddha's fenced-in fig tree decorated with oranges and prayers in Bodhgaya. The small clump of wind-blasted irises huddled beneath a thin shelf of stone on *Cerro de la Muerte*. The tracks of a green sea turtle descending the olive-colored sand down to the swirling surf of the Caribbean. White-crowned parrots chattering a ruckus across the sun-flecked sky at dusk. We search out beauty, then, because it allows us to occupy and define the world—the colonizing mind at work.

But then Kant was a homebody. Never traveled much. Never left Prussia, and hardly left Königsberg. If beauty is in the mind of the observer, why go to the ends of the earth to search it out? Maybe, as Thoreau says, *It is not worth the while to go round the world to count the cats in Zanzibar.*

IV.

The next morning the students and I are back in the boat again on the way to a long hike in the rainforest and looking for neotropical otters along the way. Yesterday's clouds have been pushed out by a strong eastern wind and, even early, the sun is punishingly hot. It hits our bodies with a kind of slap, a hot continuous smack across our faces and our bare arms. We are less than 10° above the equator and the sunlight is ten times as powerful as it is in North America. The air still humid, the sky brilliant and blue. We move into a new channel, narrow and threatened with mangrove and sea grape. The water, the color of onyx, reflects perfectly the sky above and the variegated green of the channel ahead. We move through a tunnel of trees and sky, slowly and quietly, hoping to come around a corner and find an otter sunning on a deadfall limb.

"Otter," Luis calls suddenly and immediately cuts the motor. The boat drifts. A bare limb juts out over the water, ringed with water hyacinth. All I can see are the ripples where the otter dropped into the water. We pull up closer and wait, holding on to the surprisingly tough shoots of hyacinth. Silent, we wait. There's some movement in the mangrove roots along the bank, but we can't see anything. Five minutes. The otter has probably gone to ground. Ten minutes. Nothing. Suddenly a Jesus Christ lizard shoots off the low branches of the deadfall where it sat perfectly camouflaged and unnoticed and skips across the surface of the water with a whirligig of jade legs to the cover of the far riverbank.

"Now that was a nice surprise," says Luis.

§

Two hours later, far up river from our camp, itself hours upriver from the closest city, we start up the trail into the old growth. At the boat dock we clamber through the red mud and up the riverbank to the trailhead—a small, pistachio-green science station with its rusted red roof draped with the fingered shadows of banana fronds, and the cleared yard filled with the waste of a human presence that has nowhere to go. Hammocks hang between balsa trees in the ratty pergola, and old propane tanks and fifty-gallon plastic drums hold rainwater and garbage along the edges of the building.

Through the dim, dim, forever dim understory as the old growth towers above us we hike, Luis in front, the students in the middle, and me trailing behind, as usual. We travel deep into the towering sameness of the canopy that holds the hottest of the midday sun at bay. The tall tree trunks spangled with philodendrons, their broad leaves hollowed out in strips like slotted spoons. The forest feels oddly uniform beneath the canopy. The path we follow is a winding line of fallen leaves in a plentitude of same. The even dark of the understory spreads away from us in every direction through the gloom. The tallest of the trees—kapok, wild almond, braziletto, mahogany—parasol out broad awnings of leaves high above us to gather as much light as they can, their smooth trunks unmarked by low branches, leaving the lower forest shrouded and murky, bright noon turned to a forever dusk. Most of the life of the rainforest—humming and buzzing and hissing and silent—lives in this third, this shadowed crepuscular space where day and night blend. The life here is in constant competition for the energy that comes from that powerful sun, and, as in most places, competition can be dangerous.

We trudge for hours through the twilight of the rainforest day with little to see or hear except trogons in the distance hooting at us and an agouti rooting around for food on the forest floor. At the apogee of the hike—our trail now looping back toward the science station, towards the boats, toward comfort and ease—we cross a moss-grown nurse log dropped across the trail that hosts a thrumming mess of life in its rain-woven campus. It fell long ago and now new shoots of life reach for the sun like a series of fingers climbing perpendicularly from its decaying body. Fungus and saplings and insects, life as rich and green as the moss smeared along its side. The girls hoist themselves up and over the deadfall and pass on, following in a quiet train, straining their necks to check for monkeys moving through the canopy high above.

I am the last to cross the log and, by then, I guess the wasps have had enough. They swim out from a quiet hole in the tree and assault my back and sides and face. They churn and sing their high whine and send me at a throbbing, panicked run down the piebald path, the slight light through the canopy flashing like series of semaphores. These *tsawaim* wasps plunge out and swarm me, driving their venom into my face and scalp, the pain like plentiful scalpels, sharp and precise and multiple. They sting and sting. I scream and run. Over and over they sting, until I am a hundred yards from their tree, doubled over and heaving for breath, until I am no longer a threat or annoyance. My face throbs. My neck, my back beat with pain and heat. But the worst is yet to come.

§

And yet and yet, we keep trying. We regularly name and rename the world, I think. We define landscape and place in terms that suggest we know exactly what it is we are talking about. We articulate meaning about landscapes and cities (as well as our connection to them) in fragments of thought and sense that feel complete as the wide world of our ignorance swirls outside the windows of our comprehension. We define the rainbow piece by piece, color by color, as it hits the water hard here off the beach in Tortuguero, for example, with a spray of light that's almost physical—a wind rich and horizontal from the west as rain tears at the gnarled waves, the coconut froth and the ratty, wet raffia in the soup of the surf. At the ocean's edge, which feels like a kind of conclusion to the clumsy whisper of names we read onto the land—hummock, tussock, beach, spit, strand—we are left with no words for the choppy shove of the waves, the ache they leave on the sand slipping away. Lianas, waree palm, mahogany. The estuary hums with the tongues of many rivers including one named *Suerte*, Luck, as the blue jeans frog, thumbnail small in the tannin muck and fishtail palms, trills its delicate Morse.

All that language funnels up like heat out of the steaming earth as the sun returns; yet it is awkward, somehow, this business of naming. We live in a physical, concrete world, yes, but we live in the words we use as well—in the tension and electricity between the two—so what can I make of this opulence: the physical world and its counter-balanced cosmos of words? How can I read this physical world through the Linnaean parataxis of genus and species, and then again through the triple lens of three languages— English, Spanish, and the Latin running underneath it all like the electric life of the dead? How can I write it? How can I talk about a place if the words I use to define it keep slipping away? I try and try and such efforts hold for a while in the wind, the wind off the ocean as it breaks apart the clouds and opens a small gap for the sun to muscle through.

Nearby, a large brunette bird with a golden tail whistles and pops as it hunts in the crown of palms. In Spanish it's *oropéndola de Montezuma* (Montezuma's golden pendulum) and the sound of the Latin is pure gold: *Psarocolius Montezuma*. It barks and hisses a sound like radio static. It almost falls from the branches as it torques its body into every call. Tonight, green sea turtles will return to nest on this coastline named for them: Tortuguero means place of the turtle. Heads down in the wracked sand, they will labor at their nests and dig with winged, inarticulate hands. Tortuga verde—*Chelonia mydas*. The green sea turtle. So many names. So many meanings. Their owlish eyes will tear up in the dusty air as they excavate the deep pits in the sand, pits they will fill with their luminous eggs, white as dirty pearls in the dark. Behind them, sea oats toss their blond hair. No lights shine along the beach so as to protect the nestlings from confusion, so the turtles can see little beyond sand tented with driftwood and ruin. They gasp with beaked mouths as if drowning in the incomprehensible surf of the wind.

§

The diaspora of wasp venom travels through my body, up the multiple rivers of my bloodstream and leaves me suddenly shaking and cold and desperately needing to piss. Then the rainforest starts to tremble, fishtail palms kick their fins in the green welter beneath the canopy, and red splotches flush across my arms, my neck, my sweat-licked face. The trees spin in kaleidoscope whirls and a gray mist floods in from the edges of my eyes. I stumble after the group in a haze, literally. I am walking in a fog that only I can see. The understory is fluid and gray. I am underwater in the heavy, humid air. My head burns and throbs with my banging pulse. Each beat of my heart spreads the wealth of the wasp venom deeper into me. All I can feel is my pulse and the pain, the heat on my skin where the welts burn in silence. The rainforest flows—that's the best way to describe it—it flows and shakes and is liquid in my eyes.

My breath tightens and my heart pounds in my throat. And then come the chills. I am cold—oh so cold!—in the oven of the understory with its humidity equal to the day's ninety-five degrees. Through the sweltering rainforest I walk shaking and shivering as if through my own private winter. The group is far ahead and I stumble after them, sweat heaving off my face, the bright maps of hives rising up like watermarks across my neck and back.

I have no sense, stunned and numb, that my throat is close to closing, not even when my tongue goes dumb and swells like a river fat with flood and I am reduced to a burbling incoherence. Even with a tongue grotesquely large in my mouth, even with that fat slug of muscle close to blocking my windpipe, I have no thought that the last sight I'll see will be a green shriek of light carried through the trees. I walk in ignorance. My death is an unthought thought. I am all haze and chill, a stupor of venom and sweat. There is nothing to do but walk, keep moving, back to the boats, back to the lodge. One foot down, then the other. Walking will save me. Follow the bright shirts of the students before me, those splashes of cyan and lemon in the muted daylight of the understory. Follow them, step by step out of the twilight, out of the swirling liquid of the rainforest.

§

At first, for many of the students it was less than cool to care about the world unfolding before their eyes, but now, in a world so suddenly new and full of menace, power, beauty, and secrecy, that drive to see, to discover, and to know is rising to the top. Their trepidation has given way to enthusiasm, their aloof disdain to eagerness. They have suddenly taken to borrowing my guidebooks. The small ground anoles around the lodge spur a couple of girls to interest. They chase one around the walkways and through the coarse grass. The great-tailed grackle and *oropéndola de Montezuma* get appreciative audiences for their marvelous calls (loud popping whistles and raucous chatter) even though they're common birds that prosper by living off the fringes of human habitation—much as pigeons, starlings, and crows do in North America.

The girls watch with a kind of awe as chestnut-mandibled toucans, called in Spanish *Dios-te-dé* (God give you) for the sound of their call, stream through the trees behind the lodge. Their bright gold breasts and bi-colored bills flash against the overwhelming green of this barrier island. Gregarious, they move in small flocks chattering to one another, flying between the heights of stilt-rooted palms. In the trees they look cartoonish, unbalanced, their huge beaks swinging about like scythes, but in flight they arrow ahead, tail feathers perfectly balancing their huge, pointed beaks.

In one of his books, Edward O. Wilson defines a subconscious, natural, and genetic attraction of life to life that all humans share: *biophilia.* This *biophilia* is a byproduct of evolution, he argues, and helps explain why we are attracted to certain aspects of the natural world. *Biophilia* is what I see in the students as they chase anoles around the poolside, trying to identify them. *Biophilia* is what I see in them as they gather in the garden, necks strained back, marveling at the gathering of toucans in the date palm. For Wilson, it is not Plato's echo of the divine that we see in the natural world, nor Kant's potent power of perception, but rather the biological connection and fundamental unity we share with other living creatures that, in fact, helps sustain us and our human lives. Plants and creatures connect with us at a very direct and intimate level because we are already connected at a genetic and biological level. The double helix of DNA that we share across the organic spectrum means we are all linked, or—as John Muir famously says—*hitched to everything else in the Universe.* This hitching Muir talks about, this natural and unconscious connection between living beings seems true to me, both literally and figuratively. So let me say again something I said before, only more clearly. We connect with places and creatures *through metaphor* at a very direct and intimate level because we are already connected to them *physically* at a genetic and biological level. Metaphors are how the mind expresses its relationship to nature, the same way that organic life is how DNA expresses its relationship to the universe. We find meaning because we seek it, and are it. We see resemblance because we resemble.

Down at the dock, Adrienne and Mo watch a ringed kingfisher make repeated dives from an overhanging breadfruit tree, fishing for minnows. A large dramatic bird with a ragged head-crest, heavy bill for spearing fish, and a vivid band of white around its neck, it rises from the water, sparkling in the late afternoon light, with a silver fingerling slapping in its bill. The bird twists and flips its head and swallows the fish whole. The girls cheer.

§

Hours later, the chill and heat and venom wash out of me in sweat and a bone-deep shaking, and the landscape, finally, tumbles back to form. Far beyond aid, perhaps I should have made my peace, prepared myself and waited for the infinite to break through the canopy in a spray of green-gone-gold. But what did I know? Unprepared, I was not ready to face that final, simple fact of the natural world, which is threat and death. Our deaths. My death. I was not guilty of any trespass. The wasps stung for nothing I had done, really. All the others had crossed the log before me and been left alone. The threat of my death is not consequence or result, it simply is. There was no way for me to prepare for the fact of the wasps inside the dark secret lair of their hive. There is no lesson here, no shining epiphany to be found on this rugged loop through the distant and primordial world. Death is simply the aftermath of living.

In the end, nothing came of this. In the end, of course, my throat stayed open and the canopy closed. It's the distance out from our lodge—the gas lamps lit in the shifting dark, the house macaw patrolling the piered walkways, little chevrons flashing on his shoulders—that makes it really menacing. We were too far from help, any real help, to make a difference. If my throat had closed, if just a few more *tsawaim* had found me and placed their venom so carefully inside my skin, that would have been the end of the story. The end of my story.

I was in the rainforest to learn and to discover, to advance beyond the safe horizon and come back with something to say. To learn a new language of place. And what did I know now? What was I learning? When Elizabeth Bishop asks that terrible question at the end of her poem "Questions of Travel," the question that I have used as an epigraph for this whole tale of traveling woe, when she asks whether we should have just stayed at home, she already knows the answer. The answer is *No. We should not have stayed at home.* She asks the question even as she leaves. Bishop the traveler. Bishop the wanderer. Bishop who steps off a boat in Brazil on her trip around the world and almost dies. Bishop who stays there in the rainforest, tied to that place by her love for another young woman (Lota de Macedo Soares), but tied eventually, too, by her love and fascination for this rich, new landscape. This neotropical rainforest.

The world is made anew for infant eyes and a fresh mind. That's the theory, right? That's what we are doing here in Costa Rica, why I have brought these students into a new world. The language of the rainforest is one of beauty and beneficence—that's the popular view, and one I admit to encouraging here on this course with my students, the view that sees place as a luminous product to be consumed—but inside that beneficence lives very real and very serious hazard. Novelty allows us to see more clearly, but what worth is novelty when threat lives deep inside it? The edges of the untraveled path are lined with fer-de-lance, sleeping the heat of the day away in the blossom of their perfect camouflage. Silent trees are heavy with hives of wasps.

Yes, there is threat. Yes, there is danger. Elizabeth Bishop nearly died in Brazil and Lota Soares nursed her back to health. She could have gone home; she would have had a good reason to do so. Still, it would have been a pity for her not to see the spattered sunlight scribbled down to nothing more than matchlight on army ants engraving paths in the leaf litter across the trail, as I have seen. It would have been a pity for her not to have read the cuneiform of tapir prints in the mud of the seeping stream that funnels, as it does here, into the Amazon. Or seen the wattled jacana that has just now waddled across great green platters of the water lilies with her vast, forked feet. It would have been a pity never to have pulled piranha from the river and watched them slap their gibberish across the bottom of the boat. It would have been a pity never to have found the remains of a saddleback tamarin on an old log, a slur of fur and black fingers, and understood them (as I do now) to be the fact of a jaguar ranging in the night, or seen a troupe of the world's smallest monkey—the pygmy marmoset—chatter like chipmunks from the one tree—yes, that one tree there, at the edge of the path—where they live their whole lives and never leave. Yes, it would have been a pity.

§

The students and I leave Tortuguero early the next morning in a powerful rainforest downpour, loading our gear into two small planes on a wet strip of tarmac carved into the scrub of the barrier island. The small plane bucks and jumps as we rise off the ground and pass quickly through the clouds, the green expanse of the park cut through with the dark veins of rivers vanishing into the mist. As the clouds break below us, we rise toward the highlands and the mountains beyond. On the mountain slopes, farmland takes over the landscape, rectilinear and constrained. Banana plantations. Pineapple in long, spiky rows, like aloe. Orchid farms, their fields covered in black plastic netting to simulate the forever twilight of the rainforest floor. Rain bleeds off the windows as we rise into a slice of open air between the clouds. Suddenly the light hits us from behind and we are flying directly through a rainbow that completely circles the plane. A full-throttle ring of deep indigo transforming across the full spectrum, color by color, to carmine. *Dios-te-dé* indeed.

V.

Back in San José, in the city with its careful rectangles of life, its noise and its traffic, garbage in the tall gutters. Back in San José, back in the bus, we pass the bars and the department stores, the low-slung cinderblock houses with their woven roofs of ceramic tile on our quick way out of town. Back north, up the Pan-American Highway, past the casinos and the car dealers (now muted and drab and a little sad in the light of day) toward the Pacific. We are heading for Monteverde, a famous private reserve high in the cloud forest of the Pacific Slope. Only 200 kilometers away, it will take us four and a half hours to get there. So we have some time to kill.

"The Monteverde Cloud Forest Reserve is a small, private mountain reserve of only 10,500 hectares, locked in by fog and clouds most of the time," I tell the students as we rattle up the road out of the city. The bus is the best time for me to lecture. They are my captive audience. I am standing at the front, holding tight to the luggage racks and swaying back and forth as the bus careens from pothole to pothole.

"Moisture-rich air blows in off the Pacific and as it rises (the reserve sits between 1,200 and 1,880 meters) it cools and condenses, leaving the trees laved in a perpetual mist. Epiphytes (ferns, bromeliads, orchids, or mosses), plants that take no nutrients from the soil, abound in this cloud forest. *Epiphyte* means, literally, living on or growing in the air." These plants take all the nutrients they need from the tropical air—water from the rain and mist and earth, amazingly enough, from dust and airborne dirt, whatever they can catch in their cup-like flowers and nets of aerial roots. Small as fingernail orchids or large as philodendrons with leaves the size of platters, they grow on but do not parasitize the trees. "Several species of strangler fig are common here as well. You've seen those before, in Tortuguero." Stranglers begin as epiphytes but quickly send out woody roots to the forest floor. These roots spread out and encircle the host tree, eventually killing it. When the host tree dies and rots away, what remains is the shell of the fig's thick roots with an airy, hollow center. Loaded down themselves with epiphytes, and often bent at odd angles by their own weight and the lack of internal support, mature strangler figs resemble not so much trees as gargantuan, communal organisms. A curtain of roots topped with a wild hair of ferns, moss, philodendrons, and bromeliads.

Outside the city, we are back in the countryside of small farms and roadside cafes—the highway is busy and slow. Tourist shops sell swales of hammocks, colorful as parrots, and the fruit stands are lined with pyramids of papaya and small green heads of watermelon, hanging racks of banana and plantain mottled green and a dull yellow. The air smells warm—like asphalt and burnt sugar.

"That's just what it is," says Luis. "Every year, the farmers they burn they fields of sugarcane"—the word comes out like *chugarcane*. "Clears out the rats and the dead plants. Snake too. That's what you smelling."

"Snake?" Chihiro asks, looking up from her journal.

Luis smiles his wide smile, broad as a billboard. His thin moustache. "Of course. Lots of snake in there. They like it. Places to hide, lot of rats. Perfect for snake."

She shudders and puts her face back in her book.

Down and down we go. The road twisting switchback after switchback, around the low hills, crossing bridges suspended over gorges of small streams runneling the hills. Down through towering *allées* of Flame of the Forest, tall trees like oaks with canopies blanketed with orange blossoms. Down, finally to horse pasture and dry grass. Living fence. Across Costa Rica farmers plant fence-lines of cut branches of the *poró de cerca* tree and the soil is rich enough that the tree branches root quickly and grow into fences of trees lined with barbed wire along the dusty roadside.

The Pacific coast of Costa Rica is as different from the Caribbean as Northern California is from Florida. Mountainous and rugged with rolling foothills rising to volcanic peaks perpetually wreathed in streamers of cloud. Down low, dry grasses and dusty eucalyptus trees dominate. These farm-covered hills beyond the bus windows resemble Northern California, in a way, I think. Northern California with palm trees and mango plantations. Northern California with parrots streaming through the blue-gray mottle of the cloud-filled sky. By now most of the students are asleep or zoned out—no longer listening to me and my ramblings about place, so I am left alone with my thoughts.

At this elevation the deciduous forest of the lowlands (many trees lose their leaves in the dry season) has given way to a dense evergreen forest washed by the mists of the low Pacific clouds. Farmland and cultivation decorate the slopes of the *Tilarán Cordillera* as the hills roll down toward the Gulf of Nicoya. Farmhouses dot the ridgelines and the living fences line the roadsides. A perfect, tropical pastoral. *The pastoral.* When I name the world this way I evoke a set of images and ideas about the land that go back thousands of years. That image of shepherds and their sheep grazing safely on the wide green of cleared land, that blended space between city and the wilderness, the ease of the garden and the well-turned field, safety, home. The risk and danger of wild nature is opposed to the human city's corruption and decadence. Humans seem to find a kind of perfection in the generous, welcoming landscape of the in-between, the sheep-fold and meadow, the pasture: the word pastoral encompasses all this. And despite the expectation of Costa Rica as an exemplar of raw wilderness, the image of the pastoral is essential to what we are doing here in this national-park surrounded farmland.

That word *pastoral* brings me back to Keats and his nightingale. When Keats talks about his nightingale—*light-winged Dryad of the trees...* who...*Singest of summer in full-throated ease*—that bird and the world it creates with its song represents a perfect pastoral space floating out ahead of him, forever receding. The world of the bird is a kind of nature, but it is also the poetic world and the world of ease and comfort. It is *Flora and the country green, Dance, and Provençal song, and sunburnt mirth!* It is southern warmth and the countryside, as opposed to the cold rigor and grid of the urban space of London, say, or San José. It is a kind of upper-class luxury, too, for who else uses the "country green" for leisure and mirth? The pastoral is a space we are very familiar with—comfortable in, even—because the image and idea of the pastoral has, in fact, been a fundamental and necessary trope in western thought since its Greek inception. It begins long ago with the work of Theocritus, who began the idea by writing about the rustic life of Sicily for the sophisticates in the city of Alexandria. But more importantly, by driving a wedge between the articulation of civilization and technology that reaches its apotheosis in the city and the untamed rough abundance and opulence of the wilderness, the pastoral names the space where most of our imaginative and physical lives have been and continue to be lived. Well, mine at least. The pastoral, then, is the landscape of comfort and ease that we long for, that we try and build from the rough wood of the wilderness, and hope past hope that it holds.

And of course it is in a bird that Keats finds the ultimate resemblance for that pastoral longing. Birds are symbols of the holy, of the spirit, and of that which flees from us. They are light and grace and color, permanent ease in a green world, and we chase them and catalogue them (once with guns and taxidermy, but now mostly with the eye alone, with binoculars and the long rifle of the spotting scope). This bird, the nightingale, is central to the world Keats wants us to see, his opiate world, his gauzy Eden. But what's funny is we never see the bird. Keats never sees it. The nightingale hides away in the underbrush, singing its song of comfort and summer. The song of the bird resembles the world it lives in, the grace of safe nature, but at the same time, the pastoral elegance of the bird's song is a mirage, a will-o'-the-wisp drawing us deeper into the raucous wealth of the natural world that ever recedes from us.

We turn off the main road and start climbing again. It is a bird we are climbing to see today, too, a famous bird, a glorious, mythical bird of green and crimson. We are driving out from the city to look for the resplendent quetzal. The students and I ascend the famously difficult road to Monteverde, climbing through several different ecosystems—dry ranchland giving way to transitional forest like African chaparral and finally the cloud forest with its skin of moss laved in continuous mist—the landscape greening by the kilometer as we ascend. The road is rough and potholed and tricky even in the dry season—it's murder in the rainy season, apparently. The bus swerves and veers and bangs and lurches across the ruts and washouts. I ask Manuel, our driver, if he has ever slid off the road, and his answer comes quickly and without hesitation. *Claro.* Of course.

§

Emerald green with a dramatic ridge crest, streaming tail feathers that flash green-gold in the late light of day, and a crimson chest: this is the resplendent quetzal. The quetzal is one of the most sought after birds in the world—a life-list all-star. For the Mayans, the quetzal symbolized the moment of creation and the will of the creator come to earth; his flight through the trees—like a wobbling sine curve—evokes the give and take, life and death cycle of the universe. And, in fact, the 1,100 year-old temple of the Kukulcan, in Chichén Itzá, may be acoustically designed to mimic the ascending-descending call of the quetzal. A fast clap of hands at the base of Kukulcan's staircase and a "chirped echo" follows —a *chirr-roop* like the cry of the quetzal. Along with jade, quetzal tail feathers were among the most valuable commodities of the Mayan empire; they adorned the robes of kings and priests. But this bird is also a marker of sorrow and loss. The quetzal's mythology testifies that the bird received its bright red chest only after the conquest of the Americas. As the story goes, during the invasion of the Spaniards, and after a horrific battle where thousands of Mayans died, a flock of birds descended onto a battlefield to weep over the fallen, staining their chests in the blood of their worshipers. They carry that color still in remembrance.

§

"Monteverde is rich in biodiversity, beyond the imagination of most of us," I keep going. My mini-lecture as we trundle and weave up the road that is often nothing more than a collection of ruts woven into the forest and hemmed in by ditches. "The park is home to 400 species of birds and 300 kinds of orchid. More than 3,000 plant species make their home in the reserve and there are more types of tree here—across 300 square kilometers—than in all of North America. 100 species of mammals and 120 reptile and amphibian species. 750 species of butterfly and 138 species of dragon/damselfly. Biologists found more than 500 *species* of beetle on one single tree. But it is also known, famously, as the habitat of the golden toad (*Bufo periglenes*), a species that hasn't been seen since 1989. Toads and amphibians are indicator species. They are extremely sensitive to changes and chemicals in their environment, and their dramatic decline across the globe indicates the precarious position of many species in the face of human encroachment and habitat loss." Outside the bus windows, moss greens the tree trunks and bromeliads and epiphytes line the branches that lean out over the road. Trees like hoary old men, bearded with moss and living plants.

"Species figures alone suggest that humans have encountered and named only twenty five percent of the earth's biodiversity; 5-7 million plants and animals (primarily invertebrates) remain unknown and species loss in the next hundred years is estimated at 50%—that is, half the world's known species are expected to be extinct by 2100, the largest mass extinction since the Cretaceous-Tertiary that leveled the dinosaurs and welcomed in the age of mammals. Those that survive this extinction will be those that are most like us—squirrels, pigeons, rats, cockroaches, coyotes, white-tailed deer, grackles—generalists, adaptable to multiple ecosystems, tolerant of garbage, waste, and ruin. In other words, we know almost nothing about the world we live in. And most of what we know (and do not know) will vanish before our closed eyes over the course of the next century."

The girls are tuning me out. I can see it. They fade; their eyes drift to the windows and the floating ghostly world outside. It's hard. I get it. The experience of nature is not the same as the discussion of the experience of nature. And worse. The complexity of the interactions of species in a well-studied ecosystem lies far outside the ability of human science and knowledge to fully understand it. Even the system of Linnaean taxonomy—that architecture of knowledge we have created to define and catalogue the world, that system we depend on to name and define the articulate natural word outside our doors—even that taxonomy adjusts and amends itself, almost daily, to accommodate new understandings, new discoveries, new species. This world is both fragile and hard to see.

§

A member of the Trogon family, the quetzal is the size of a large parrot and feeds mainly on fruits and berries, which the bird plucks as it hovers. In Costa Rica, the birds are especially fond of figs and wild avocados. For the most part, quetzals sit motionless in the high trees, elegant, as if posed. During spring courtship, however, males launch from the crowns of hundred-meter trees, circle in song, and then rocket down, tails streaming like a comet's. Just before striking the earth, the male will pull out of his dive and alight next to his audience—a female bird. If the female is impressed—if the ascent is high enough and the descent sufficiently shallow—they will make their nest together. This is the beauty of sexual selection, of fitness measured by extravagance.

§

Our lodge lies on the edge of the cloud forest, a tension zone between the dry forest and the clouds, halfway between the raw material of the wilderness and the cities down below that dot the sun-speckled valley. A green metal roof and 80s ski-lodge architecture meet beneath the slight wind that blows clouds and mist that accumulate as they rise up the hills. Weirdly, here, the sun shines at the same time as a mist fills the air. Look up, blue sky. Look east, up the mountains, clouds and swirling fog. Look west, sunlight falling on the green hills as they drop down into the Gulf of Nicoya.

With a few of my students—Mo and Adrienne, and even Chihiro who has found some sense of adventure that wasn't there three days ago at the bottom of her deep well of caution—I take horses out into the farmland, through open pasture and on to the lookout point. We wander through farms and cross a small gap out through the living fence on to back roads of mud and dust. The Gulf of Nicoya spreads out below us in a lace of islands and the mountains of the distant peninsula line up on the horizon. The sunlight is opalescent and pours through the broken clouds in solid shafts of pearl. It hits the water below and the gulf gleams like molten silver. Small slivers of rainbow stripe the nearby peaks, tucked into their beds of green.

The guide clucks at the horses and leads us up into the hills, aiming for a gap in the forest that looms ahead like a small storm. We tie up the horses and open a branch-and-wire gate leading to a short trail through the woods and emerge into a clearing with a small wooden house and garden. The house is dilapidated but carefully tended, a kind of strange juxtaposition of decay and attention. The worn wood walls are gray and streaked with bands of moss and the rafters appear to be halfway rotted under the palm-thatched roof. Across from the garden, a line of large, hutched cages closed with chicken wire. The cages hold orphaned animals—coati, a paca (a large, nocturnal rodent)—whose parents were killed or lost. A small wild pig and two aggressive swans roam freely about the hardpan of mud that circles the house. But the monkeys, white-faced capuchins, the monkeys are what the girls want to see. Two juveniles rattle around on the tin roof of the cages. Seeing us, the capuchins chatter and squeak. Small monkeys, all black except for their white faces and shoulders. Their eyes are petite and expressive, their hands and feet dark and leathery with jet-black nails. They make teeth-sucking sounds, like a sequence of quick kisses. Slowly, they swing down from the corrugated eaves and onto the outstretched hands of the girls. The larger one scampers up onto Mo's head. The monkey is all over her, pulling at her sunglasses and biting her hair. Her face is grimace and wince. The capuchin starts to groom her hair, and she follows his gesture, petting his soft-yet-tenacious tail. A primate bonding session.

"Dude," says Adrienne, her voice low with rough astonishment. "You have *a monkey* on your head."

§

The pastoral is a fundamentally human landscape, controlled and defined by our needs, I write in my journal, back in the lodge and warming the chill of the night forest from me in front of the large fire set in the circular fire-pit. Feet up, chair tilted back. My body soaking in the warmth. The bar around me murmurs with a kind of quiet contentment. There is a deeply felt pastoral welcome designed into this lodge. The pastoral is both a place for safety and comfort and the craving to access that space of safety and repose to begin with. Even, here, in places like this, in parks and nature reserves, in places where the wild is supposed to predominate, these landscapes we enter are for the most part scaled down representations of a primordial world that was once far more rich with risk, beauty, and wonder than anything we encounter regularly today. We enter daily "an abstract wild," to use Jack Turner's phrase, a wild devoid of threat but also of the full opulence that once lived on the planet. This loss represents a staggering destruction of biodiversity—primarily from habitat loss—but also from the human tendency to simplify nature, to make it readable and workable to the human eye, to turn wilderness into garden, to turn garden into city and suburb.

The idyllic pastoral hillside that sleeps now beyond these large windows, resting on its back in the dark, the soft swell of farms rolling down the foothills to the Pacific, the pastoral with its blend of simplicity and sophistication, where the artifice of the city blends with the untamed energy of the wilderness, such is the imaginative landscape of much traditional, western thinking about place. I write this all down in my journal, battered and wet with loose pages and plane tickets jutting out. But at the same time, I am thinking that the pastoral feels like a fantasy. Or perhaps fantasy is the wrong word. The pastoral is so deep inside our conception of place that we cannot see it any more. It is our image of the world *and* the very structure of that image. The illusion that the pastoral has gone missing, that it is just an old-fashioned *Little House on the Prairie* trope that carries no weight any more, represents its most radical victory. Instead of being *what* we imagine the world to be, it is in fact *how* we imagine the world to be. It is the way we imagine, always present yet unaccounted for in our thoughts. And despite the illusion that the pastoral has for the most part lost its hold on contemporary thinking, I am certain that it remains a dominant trope in modern thought, despite (or perhaps because of) its ability to subtly reinforce certain political and social narratives about nature and the human relationship to the land.

§

The next morning Luis and I take the class out early into a hard wind and the park itself. The towering cloud forest exists in our minds—in the conventional wisdom—as a labyrinth of misted trees, each with its own resident animal: birds and jaguars, butterflies and monkeys. A green refuge for the world's haunted and hunted biodiversity. It does look like that. A bit. But today, the cloud forest is wet and noisy and it's impossible to see any animals at all. The wind in the branches and the cold rain turns the forest inwards. We can see only feet ahead of us and it makes for a miserable hike. Chihiro is grumbling again, but then, too, so are many of the others—wet in their raingear, their heads down. We see the epiphytes and bromeliads, the remarkable architecture of the strangler figs, but nothing else. The forest is dark, thick, and everywhere in motion. Rain ticks off the fat leaves. Lianas quiver and twitch. Branches toss in the wind. We cannot find the quetzal. They are hiding, stuffed into woodpecker holes, and so is everything else with any brains. We are out and underdressed. Miserable.

The girls and I cross the long suspension bridge at the heart of the park, the springing metal holding us up 50 meters above the small creek below. The sides of the ravine are steep and ferociously green. Thicker undergrowth throws up a few large trees, ceiba and fig, spangled with epiphytes. Directly below us, the tree ferns look like green stars. The mist swirls below our feet and above our heads; the trees disappear in the heavy air. We can see the metal lattice of the bridge below our feet stretching off in two directions, suspending us high in the white air. Kapok trees appear and disappear like reverse ghosts in the distance, dark shadows of life amidst the gauzy abundance. The clouds come in heavy off the Pacific, rising up into this ravine and filling it with cold shadows. There is nothing to see, nowhere to go. We are orphaned and alone on the bridge, hanging on to the railing as the world turns white and the forest vanishes. We never find the quetzal.

§

Manuel Antonio. That's our next stop. When I arrived here with Dave and my mountain bike ten years ago, it was a sleepy beach town next to a national park of incomparable beauty. And some things haven't changed. The park itself still lies in that beautiful sequence of scalloped coves between headlands—*Punta Quepos* and *Punta Cathedral*—for example. The beach is still lined with sea grape towered over by wild avocados and the poisonous manchineels. (In Spanish, the manchineel is called the *little apple of death*.) Just off the point, a series of small rock outcrops and islands still jut from the ragged ocean, supporting nesting colonies of brown boobies, terns, and magnificent frigate birds. But between my visits, the world has found this place. Today the road to Manuel Antonio from Quepos along the beach is lined with hotels and new casinos; there's a restaurant in a C-130 cargo jet out on the point and, down below, another built in old railroad cars. Signs advertise Internet access, ESPN, and CNN. Ten years ago, there was one bar and a restaurant down on the beach, *Mar y Sombra*, where—if you remember—I endured the biggest earthquake to hit Costa Rica in recorded history, 7.6 on the Richter Scale. That day, the world shook hard and everything turned fluid. I remember it fondly (the bar, not the earthquake). Now there are ten bars and as many hotels and Manuel Antonio is heir to all the problems of beach towns everywhere—overcrowding and pollution, surfers and stoners, parked cars and hustlers. There's even a disco.

§

I go back to Jack Turner, pulling his book from my bag, to think more fully about this connection between place and the pastoral. The pastoral may help us reconnect with the natural world, to cross the boundary between the human domain and world outside our walls, but it is not a natural landscape. It is safe. It is comfortable. It is accessible. And it is built, a model, a mockup, a text that we both write and read. Manuel Antonio is the perfect Costa Rican version of this abstraction. It is a landscape of model and construct; it is a ridge of nice hotels overlooking the glorious conjoining of sea and stone, the rough earth thrust up from beneath the waves and smeared with green. It looks beautiful and wild but it is, really, neither. In other words, the pastoral attracts and compels because it *resembles* the wild. People come here to experience an imagined, constructed version of landscape—as we have done— but stay and return because they are comfortable. The true wild is difficult and dangerous. It is fragile, but it is also complicated and full of risk. So we make from the world, from its richness and fecundity, from its overwhelming plentitude, a model that resembles the natural world. We create a natural space that is accessible and engage-able—that teaches us, that makes us better people. That's the argument, my argument. That's why I have brought my students here. But in doing so we limit. We control. We settle and diminish.

We own the land, whether personally in the form of our houses and gardens and farms or socially in terms of our parks and preserves. And what's more, we don't just own the land; we consume it. The pastoral space of the park, this park, *Parque Nacional Manuel Antonio*, is a landscape designed—at all levels: recreation, relaxation, and education—for human consumption. The politics of owning land, of controlling nature and, at once, learning from it, consuming it, and gaining sustenance, tie the twin ends of the pastoral together. The land feeds us, physically of course, and linguistically, as I have argued, but it also creates a kind of political space where the owner of (and the visitor to) the land is free—free to do as she wishes and to become better than she was before. The New World, in particular, in the pastoral garden of the Americas with its blending of personal freedom and political responsibility, is where one becomes a citizen rather than a servant.

This park is just that—a model of the wild made for human consumption. Our hotel—low-slung and tucked between towering trees, its wonderful gardens of ornamental palms and heliconia frequented by scarlet-rumped tanagers, rufous-tailed hummingbirds, and yellow-crowned euphonia—backs up to the park. Bougainvillea swoops over the butter-yellow walls like breaking waves of magenta and lavender. Leather banana and fishtail palms pulled from wetter forests and replanted here thrive where they are well watered. Tejano music bangs from the speakers and swirls around the crystalline eye of the pool. We are meters from the beach, just up the road from *Mar y Sombra,* which I point out to my students with great pride. At night we watch as crab-eating raccoons and a kinkajou climb down out of the trees to drink from the fresh water in the pool. The wild is laid out at our feet, not like old-fashioned taxidermy, an image of colonialism, but in a new age, commercial trophy of enterprise, ecotourism, and commerce. This is the romantic pastoral for sale to the citizens of the new world.

In the physical transformation and occupation of the Americas, in the destruction of wilderness and the creation of a pastoral space, but equally in the creation of a new political class—the democratic citizen capable of seeking out the entertainment and the education of the natural world, the experience of the so-called wild—the American experiment evokes a political narrative out of the physical encounter with these two continents and their space and possibility. That narrative particularly depends on the belief that the pastoral landscape grants people autonomy, freedom, greatness, and, above all, knowledge. But clearly, the "wild" is the price this park paid for our knowledge.

Manuel Antonio National Park is nature subject to the dilemmas of overuse and over-knowing. The animals in the park, particularly the white-faced capuchins, have lost their fear of humans and are quite adept at scavenging garbage and even opening backpacks and other luggage in search of food. They have been known to drop from trees in front of hikers and bare their teeth, demanding the food they know all hikers carry. At the hotel, the staff leaves food out for a troupe of squirrel monkeys that comes down from the forest every afternoon to feed. Reddish-brown with black heads and white facial masks, these monkeys are the most gregarious of all the Costa Rican simians. The juveniles, especially, roughhouse through the trees in chattering clumps. They come close for photographs, gossiping and chirping like songbirds, their tiny black hands holding tight to each other. The students, though, shriek with delight at the monkeys. They want to touch them, to stroke them like cats. Chihiro approaches the pair of monkeys who crouch together on a feeder—really just an aluminum pole planted in the ground of the garden and topped with a small platform where the hotel staff leaves old fruit: mottled bananas or papaya rinds. The monkeys—two of them there on the feeding platform—hunker together like kittens as she approaches. They cock their heads, flash her their big eyes, deep and black and surrounded by the white mask on their faces. She moves in slowly, her hand raised, her dark bangs falling across her eyes. She wants to touch a monkey, I know, but no good can come of this. I watch her from my patio. One step closer, two. The monkeys shriek and squeal and hiss— all at once really, that's what it sounds like—and leap for the branches of the mango tree above their heads. Chihiro shrieks and leaps back, too.

§

My students and I have moved from the wilder space of Tortuguero, a landscape inaccessible by anything but boat and still very remote, to Manuel Antonio, a diminished wild, an abstract wild. The semblance of the wild that is being sold at Manuel Antonio depends on both access to animals and the natural beauty of the place. But by becoming overly accustomed to human presence the animals lose the essence of wildness that makes them desirable. For example, those capuchins that regularly drop from the trees in front of hikers and bare their teeth. Or the coati—diurnal raccoons that go by many names: Brazilian aardvarks, hog-nosed coons, *pizotes, gatosolos,* crackoons, and snookum bears—coati with their pointed noses and the thin striped tails they hold aloft like cat tails who have learned to open bags left on the beach and scamper off with sandwiches and fruit. They scavenge in our refuse; they live in the wake human beings make as we move through the world.

When the crowds pile up and the trash they leave, when the tranquil beauty of a place like this coastline draws people in numbers too high to sustain that beauty, something very real is lost in our encounter with the landscape. When the weight of people moving across the landscape damages the very landscape they have come to see, there is a real price that the natural world pays for our attraction to it. Aldo Leopold remarked that we will only save those landscapes we love, and we can only love the places we know. But the corollary of this axiom is a paradoxical problem: our very desire to know and experience a place—to be intimate with it—is often to the detriment of both. The more we know a place (and the more people who "know" it) the more it suffers from the weight and experience of our knowledge.

Perhaps we have gone in the wrong direction, my students and I, with the current of civilization and industrialization rather than against it; perhaps we should be trying the reverse path. Maybe, then, the students would have a clearer idea of what has been lost. But that path is dangerous, isn't it? There's a threat in the primordial world that demands respect and, ultimately, blocks our ability to learn from that world. What we see here in this abstract wild is a chastened, softened world. A safe world. The pastoral exists where the power of the wild is diminished and the potency of the beautiful—the form of it created by us and through us—is heightened. What we see here, in Manuel Antonio, is not the nature as it once was, a dangerous, primordial world, a world that took patience, care, and a lifetime to learn. What we see is manicured and curated. What we walk through is a garden, with a bird singing beyond sight lost in the distant trees.

VI.

The remote island in which I found myself situated, in an almost unvisited sea, far from the tracks of the merchant fleets and navies; the wild luxuriant tropical forest, which stretched far away on every side...all had their influence in determining the emotions with which I gazed upon this "thing of beauty." So writes Alfred Russel Wallace, co-founder (with Charles Darwin) of the theory of evolution and the greatest field biologist of his era. He writes from an elevated bamboo hut on Aru in the far-flung islands of the Malay Archipelago, his headquarters for the exploration of a root-crop village at the head of the Watelai River. Rainforest looms up around the village like storm clouds, but he has brought the sun with him, the natives say. Striped light pours down through the canopy. He pays his rent in cloth and axe heads, in beads and tobacco.

§

In a tight box canyon down below the stunted, waxed-grass chusquea of *Cerro de la Muerte*, the Savegre River slices its cold way through rolled boulders and splashes in pools clear as acrylic. Hummingbirds slash and chip the bright, cool air into rough territories of fragrant hyacinth and orchid. Their quick black tongues wire the blossoms from below as they hover: violet sabrewings, magnificent hummingbirds, volcano hummingbirds small as thumbs, and green violetears, whose name speaks to the smear of electric indigo that trails from the eyes of the males.

Above the Savegre valley floor, small orchards give way to oak cloud forest, gnarled and hung with bromeliads, a scarlet plant with bayonet leaves like agave. Cipresillo oak, plentiful in this valley and endemic to Costa Rica, remains in only a few other places across the country, though it once was the principal tree of montane forests until heavy logging and agriculture limited it to the steepest of canyons. The dominant trees here reach 50 meters in height, like the wild braziletto and the winter's bark tree.

The Talamanca Range rises abruptly out of the Pacific here, climbing to more than 10,000 feet in less than 80 kilometers, and its sculpted canyons capture the clouds as the moisture-laden air flows off the ocean and up the steep slopes. The clouds lave the forests with mist and produce rich mats of bromeliads, lichen, and ferns that drape over every horizontal branch and wedge into each crotch. The air is verdant and chiming with water falling from every pitched boulder. Tree ferns, prehistoric survivors, stand up in the understory, as philodendrons with hollowed-out leaves like slotted spoons (to avoid insect predation) snake up the thick, buttressed trunks of mountain needle and blueberry.

Sunlight slits through the trees and into the mist that lingers in this cloud forest, leaves so jittery with the pulse of dripping water that leaf-shadows tremble on the forest floor. A green violetear hummingbird haunts the lilac-blazed path down the canyon where in stock ponds trout rib the water with interlocking loops as they rise towards a late hatch of stonefly. The bird's incomprehensible heart hammers inside its chest.

The road down into the canyon is clearly a kind of madness, the sheer, laddered switchbacks testing the bus's gearbox as we descend past coffee plantations woven into the cliffside and the crimson *pointillisme* of the fruit against the waxy leaves, but something beautiful lives on in the oceanic color of the indigo tear that streaks that flash of emerald iridescence. And equally some kind of precise perception lives in the act of naming this bird for the ocean—*Colibri thalassinus* (*Colibri* is a hummingbird genus and *thalassian* means "pertaining to the sea")—when we are so far from the shore. By naming we connect worlds. Here, in this bird, we connect the sea's vast smear of color and power to this tiny, pugnacious dynamo of hum and flight. But by naming we tame, as well, and by reading these words we watch as through the bars of a cage. Yet there is a power in the world that lies beyond language, or rather, a power that draws us back again and again, in language, to try and corral it. There is something in the world larger than the garden we would make from it. Far below these mountains, where this valley exits into plantations of palm oil and teak and the welcoming grids of Quepos and Manuel Antonio, the surf of the clouds breaks and shatters against the sea wall of the cordillera.

§

Six months of the year in the Amazon basin, the Tahuayo River rises up around the shoulders of the trees and fish fly through hectares of flooded forest. They school in the tree branches stretched through the slow-flowing water in great flocks of scale and fin and saucer eyes while giant, bird-hunting spiders billboard webs low across the water in the shrubby canopy of flooded ceiba and cecropia. The river water, draining from the deep snow of the high Andes, can rise up to 10 meters every season.

Here, a strangler fig splays out in a skeletal fan beside wide colonnades of kapok and the white sun soon finishes off the dawn. Here, tree boas sleep tentacled above the water across a fan of leaves to avoid the crushing heat of noon and a wire-tailed manakin flames through the middle-story treetops like a little puff of fire. The seeping tannin water, deep as steeped tea, consumes the edges of the trees, and we float above and inside this flooded forest in our wooden canoe with a clicking symphony of fish sounds trickling up through the gunwales.

At night, out in the canoe upriver in the flooded forest, beneath fig trees that arch and plunge in gothic tangles, the bang and stammer of tree frogs' song orchestrates desire in this forest. One frog comes gluey off the mimosa, his eyes red as blood blisters beneath our lights. The males, like this one, sing for the females, and there is a lot of competition. Loud they are. Loud enough to fill this night with noise, fill it to overflowing. They croak and bang and whimper and tweet. An untuned orchestra, a symphony of sexual desire. They warble and chirp—songbirds for the dark hours. They rumble and groan. We float in a dark hall of sound—so loud!—its walls made of kapok and fig. A black cacophony of frog song. *Loud, loud, loud, loud!* they yell. The banging of the frogs fills the clearing where we float as if suspended in a bowl of night. The world overwhelmed with their want as the golden foil of caiman eyeshine along the banks balances the smear of stars across the sky.

§

In the Savegre cloud forest, years after my first encounter with *Cerro de la Muerte* and with a new group of students, where *Las Robles* trail staircases through mossy roots of braziletto and oak and the cloud forest is full of small streams that chime and cascade through a mossed-over landscape of green, I finally see the bird, a male. The resplendent quetzal. It has taken me ten years and four trips to Costa Rica to find this bird, this bird that now sits stoically in high branches, its chest and tail bright as red orchids in the humid air. Its call rings out—two notes, high-low: *chirr-roop, chirr-roop*— and females appear. Two of them, fluttering through backlit branches. Females lack the dramatic crest and streaming tail of the male, but they are still striking: deep emerald with a dun-scarlet chest. *Chirr-roop!* Their answers fill the valley.

§

In the lodge in Savegre, around the fire built up here at the back end of the bar—a small stove keeps the chill of the mountain night at bay beyond the framed windows—I am lecturing again. Trying to unravel, with a new group of students, this complicated cloth of beauty and grief, of nature and death, and the way the narratives we tell weave both together. But all I have are fragments and stories; I need to find a way to bind all this together. I have begun to think of all these courses, all these trips to the tropics, as one trip. I have begun to think about my stories as one unified narrative. Story and memory blend with the present and the past becomes as fluid as the misted wind flowing outside the windows.

Right now, around the fire, I am talking about some elegies I have given them to read—including, of course, Keats' "Ode to a Nightingale"—and I am trying to draw them all together here with the new world, this Rich Coast, where these students find themselves. I am trying to get them—oh, just say it! *I* am trying to think—*me, myself*—in new ways about place. I am trying to bring last year's student trip to the Amazon in Peru together with Costa Rica, in the here and now. Trying to think about Alfred Wallace adrift in the Malay Archipelago inventing evolutionary theory and thinking about beauty. Trying to think about birds. Trying to think about Keats. Trying to bring the blooming magnificence of the rainforest together with elegy and memory, the pastoral countryside with the landscape of poetry.

"Here's what I mean," I say to the students. "If language and image represent our distance from the world, and equally our connection to it—as I have been talking about—the pastoral represents a means of rejoining what has been lost. If we are separate and isolated creatures alone in a world that no longer feels quite like home, the pastoral, then, serves as a vehicle to create an imagined landscape, a word-world in which the losses or problems of the present can be transmuted into the gloss of imagined gold. And the primary loss of the human world is, of course, the loss of the human self through death. Our lives are finite in a natural world that seems infinite. Trees live on. Mountains stand against the wind. Generations of animals cycle onward in a kind of perpetual motion that appears unending. Nature is the original garden where life everlasting is found."

I point out the window, to the dark and shadowed world outside, the trees swaying in the wind that rises up from the Pacific and fills this valley at night, this world they have been crossing and re-crossing for days now. The students dutifully swivel their heads to follow my direction, see almost nothing out the dark windows, and swing back to me. They are tired—we hiked down from *Cerro de la Muerte* today—and unconvinced that poetry has anything to tell them about the world of mountains and clouds that they find themselves in.

"So, the urge to find in the natural world a commensurate landscape to repair the damage death has wrought remains one of the pastoral's dominant functions. The elegiac then represents one of the strongest and most continuous strains of the pastoral because the cultural work it accomplishes is perhaps the most necessary—the natural world, both broken and consoling, suffers loss, but at the same time it renews itself and presents the hope of life beyond life, of regeneration and the possibility of beginning anew."

They are still not convinced. Young and unacquainted with death, it is hard for them to imagine a world without themselves in it. To be fair, that's a bridge too far for most of us. But their eyes are wandering again. I am talking too much, again, not showing enough. As I speak I remember the way the great western star watches over the beach at Manuel Antonio as the sun sets. That star hovers high above the off-shore islands fringed with a lace of waves and old coral, hovers there as the sky teems with birds— boobies and frigate birds, terns and kites—and the sun plummets with remarkable velocity towards the warm welcome of the sea.

§

Here the Savegre canyon is compressed into the space between the ridgelines, and the overwhelming wealth of forest shakes around me as water drips from every leaf and light shifts through the ascending ladders of the trees. The gold-green plumage of the birds shines like the leaves of Eden, like a garden at first light, and the crimson chest of the male shines like blood or flowers in the mist. Quetzal voices resonate back and forth until the valley seems filled with their sound— *chirr-roop!* The male turns his head, the black bead of his eye following the females as they approach. They swirl around him, and then move off, leaving the blessing of their presence hanging in the air. I am dazzled by these birds, the electric emerald buzz of their plumage against the softened, gray-green of the cloud forest. The sine wave of their tail feathers as they flutter from branch to branch. The females twist off through the layers of the cloud forest, and the male follows, his emerald tail streaming out behind him like a caduceus.

§

At our feet, a line of leaf-cutter ants has torn a path into the grass down to bare earth outside the porch of the field station where we are staying in near Sarapiqui. The building is poor and low against the forest. Rain-rust leaking from the edges of the metal roof and a few plastic chairs spotting the concrete patios. This path leads 100 meters back to their nest and is as clean as a median. These ants are tearing apart the leaves of a nearby *guanacaste*; others from the same nest will travel to other trees and tear them down, leaf by leaf, often carrying pieces twelve times their own weight back to the nest. Amazingly, it is estimated that leaf-cutter ants move between 10 – 15% of the biomass in the rainforest. Back at the nest, the ants do not eat the leaf fragments. Instead, smaller workers cut the leaves into tiny pieces that are used as fertilizer for growing a fungus the ants use for food. This fungus grows nowhere else in the world and the ants eat nothing else. The fungus glows in the dark and lights the millions of citizens that live in any given nest—vast, underground cities lit with the fruits of their own labor.

§

Alfred Wallace has come to gather specimens for collections at home in Britain but, as always with Wallace, one suspects a deeper, more primal craving. His work and thought resonate with wonder. This thing of beauty he seeks at the fringe of the Empire is the remarkable genus *Paradisaea*—the bird of paradise.

98

There are forty-two species of *Paradisaea* that evolved in New Guinea, a land with abundant food and, importantly, without mammalian predators, a detail hinted at by their raucous cries, and the variety and splendor of the feathers, shields, streamers, and wires adorning them—the astonishing plumage of the males. There are birds with feathers like wires curled from their bodies in ampersands and treble clefs. Birds with the colors of oil on water—a mesmerizing rainbow of feathers. There are birds who dance and vibrate like electric toys, birds who moonwalk and jitterbug. There are birds with golden Mohawks and others with hypnotic cascades of crimson wing feathers. The very image of outrageous beauty.

§

I am having a hard time reaching my students. They are dazed and tired and all this theory about the pastoral and the place seems extraneous. It isn't though. I am convinced of that. If we take nature at face value, the easy pastoral grace of most of our landscapes, then we will be fooled because these landscapes have been designed to fool us. They are altered and safe and convenient. They are accessible and made for consumption. Trying to complicate our experience here in the natural world is my job. I know what language can accomplish, and sometimes my words don't seem quite up to the task.

I finish my lecture and the students look at me blankly. A few are scribbling in their notebooks. Most are waiting, waiting for me to finish so they can go have a drink at the bar, waiting so they can talk with their friends. They are far from me, and young. Most of them don't really believe they will die. At least I think that; although my ideas may be little more than cliché and the arrogance of age. I believe I know all about death, about dying. I tell my stories every year. The ride up to the top of *Cerro de la Muerte*. The earthquake. The wasps. I survived and stand in my own mind, in my own narratives, defiant below that lone star beaming out across the miles its beneficent light as the surf comes in like corduroy—the very fabric of kings. But this is all ego, isn't it? I am not the central wheel on which this story turns. The world isn't made for us, for me; that is what evolution tells us. I am isolated and alone and the world cares not whether I live or die. Death cannot, finally, be overcome, and to believe in the power of poetry to change something so fundamental is absurd. The painful and necessary gesture of elegy is to accept loss and to find a way out of the pattern in new stories, in new myths and narratives that don't duck the violence that lies at the heart of the system. Beneath that welcoming western star, clouds colonnade and fill with a light clean and well-traveled, come as it does across the reaches of the dark the way the wind carries across the Pacific, shoving the water before it, building it and piling it until it resembles the inevitable and its own weight crumbles and the long slide toward equilibrium begins. Each wave wears itself out as it reaches for the wrack at the back of the shore, but the star remains.

§

Like the quetzal, the beauty of the birds of paradise is an evolutionary endgame. What Wallace figured out in a stunning blaze of insight, unlike the measured and careful intellect of Darwin who methodically arrived at the same conclusion, is that the lack of predation on these islands demands another means of distinguishing genetic fitness (although neither man uses that term—gene theory won't catch up to evolution for years). The elaborate, luxuriant plumage and display of the males is pushed forward by sexual selection, by the desire for beauty and extravagance. Such beauty, really, has nothing to do with the human mind; it registers there nonetheless.

We look in on the world through a narrow window of time, our time, steadfastly believing that everything we see belongs to us. What is Plato's universe of forms, or Kant's formless form, but another model of colonization that would organize the earth under the domain of the human mind? The beauty of the world suggests an equally perfect representation in our consciousness, we think. Just like the Mayans, we speak, and the world organizes around our thoughts; we clap, and the world answers us in the voices of our gods. If we are lucky.

§

As my students and I move through the black, black, utter black of the flooded canopy of the Tahuayo drainage in our canoes, we pull the world forward into meaning with our flashlights. Bright spots of sensibility rise up as we play the beams of our lights over the forest; they rise up from out of the twisted darkness and fall back, released from our presence. As we pass, a blue-crowned trogon sits stunned and blinking beneath our headlamps: this parrot-sized bird with its striped, slate tail and chest of deep crimson, its dark blue head and bright eye ring that gives it a look of perpetual surprise.

We raise the landscape into meaning and return it damaged in our wake—it certainly feels that way, although I may be giving myself entirely too much credit. The slap of water off the paddles, the sweep and beam of our lights like tunnels churning through the dark. My very attempt to assemble this motley assortment of memories into a coherent collage damages the very world I want to talk about. Running together here are three different kinds of tropical forest—cloud forest, rainforest and the flooded forest of the Amazon basin—across two countries and two continents. The ants build their vast cities lit by the fungus they themselves grow, the quetzals swoop and glide through the moss-covered trees, and that star beams out across the waves of the beach at *Playa Espadilla,* all independent of one another and yet somehow linked together in a great living chain that I am trying to recreate here. They are isolate and inseparable. They are united and alone.

Wallace's understanding, like Darwin's, is that nature needs us not. *All living things were not made for man,* he concludes. *The cycle of their existence has gone on independently of his, and is disturbed or broken by every advance in man's intellectual development; and their happiness and enjoyments, their loves and hate, their struggles for existence, their vigorous life and early death, would seem to be immediately related to their own well-being and perpetuation alone.* This is the central and, to some, the most disturbing tenet of evolution. The natural world functions autonomously—full of rich gesture and complex interaction, violence, and, yes, beauty— but these gestures are not *made for us.* They are grown, organically, out of the millions of interactions that happen between species and their environments over eons of time. Beauty is not designed to fulfill our desire, but it exists nonetheless. Evolution proceeds through random chance and fortuitous circumstance and runs on the engine of death. We are fragile and fragmented creatures adrift in a world of impossible accident. And yet, because we have a complex and highly evolved brain, because we are able to look back on the world and render it through the magic and wonder of language, because we can abstract the world and make from it meaning, we are not fully alone. We are not isolated and divorced. We join the world with our words. These two notions—our intense investment in nature and nature's indifference—must be understood together, a kind of environmental "negative capability."

Negative capability is John Keats' famous phrase for the poet's ability of *being in uncertainties, Mysteries, doubts without any irritable reaching after fact & reason.* Image and metaphor: these tools of the poet open language to impossibilities and contradictions, the unsolvable resistance of nature and the world to our senses. Because metaphors reveal to us what we already know but may have forgotten, because they speak to us of the infinite and interconnected world, and because they demonstrate and orchestrate (at the same time) how the infinite of the world is connected to the infinite of the mind, they reveal themselves as thinking incarnate. Metaphors are a kind of linguistic magic, the ability to say that two disparate things are the same in ways that make no rational sense. Metaphors make an argument without arguing, prove themselves without proof, demand without compelling anyone. They are *being in uncertainty*.

The rational mind, finally, cannot contain enough to fully and finally comprehend and describe the whole experience of the natural world. Plato's right; only a god could do that. It is only through metaphor and image—those *irrational* tools of the poet that Plato feared—that we can cross the wall that separates us from the natural world. Only in the imagination, where beauty thrives without logical constraint, where images of nature are unified with the articulate and rational constructs of the human mind, only there can the multiple potentials of the natural world be fulfilled through human language and the world's beauty be harnessed, if only briefly, before it falls back into the rich sea of its particulars.

Nature fills us—the chill of the wind, the spiced scent of eucalyptus leaves snapping underfoot, the rich swell of air rushing off the Pacific, the green that washes down the sides of *Cerro de la Muerte* into the valley of *Río Savegre*—and we give that wealth meaning. Out of abundance, we define mountains and canyons, rainforests and watersheds. We identify park and piste, peak and valley. We walk through the world on paths we have named, as if their very names, in fact, called them into being. But harder to see is that world collapsing back on itself after we have passed. The trees gathering together. Melodious blackbirds returning with their manifold songs. Damage and distance and trauma are what we carry and the world retires from us in radiating waves, but the frogs, the frogs (*recall it now!*) they deafened us that night.

VII.

I am stuck. 390 out of the 900 birds listed in Skutch and Stiles' *Guide to the Birds of Costa Rica*. I am at 390 and stuck. I have worked hard for days now (after actually tallying up the birds I had marked in my well-worn version of the guidebook from ten years of visits to Costa Rica) getting up from 372 to almost four hundred. I have been up early almost daily and out with my friend and guide, Luis, We've been working together for the past ten years and he is consistently one of the happiest and most hard-working guys I know; although with his rough build, the thin mustache like the edge of a knife, and the multiple gold earrings that curve up his left ear, he might not look at first like the kind of guy you would want to run into in a dark corner of the rainforest.

Luis grew up in Tortuguero, off the grid (the town only got power 30 years ago), subsistence fishing and farming and hunting in the area that would become the Tortuguero National Park, that maze of rivers and canals crisscrossing the low tableland of the wet, Caribbean coast of Costa Rica. He started working as a fishing guide and boat driver for a local lodge and taught himself English by listening to the guests and the guides. He put himself through naturalist guide training and the certification program and quickly found work. He now lives in one of the most prosperous suburbs in San José with his young wife and their children. He's a walking success story for ecotourism and the benefits it can have on local communities.

Luis and I are up early with the scope and the binoculars and the heavy weight of the *Guide to the Birds of Costa Rica,* tromping around in the cool damp of a rainforest morning looking for enough new birds, enough to get me over the 400 mark. The low cabanas of the Laguna Lodge surround us, wood porches and hammocks dark and shadowed in the early morning gloom as we move through the gardens toward the stretch of woods beyond. The river at our backs runs thick and heavy, clumped with loose logs and small islands of water hyacinth, as it pushes a heavy weight of runoff toward the sea. The morning is damp but the rain has stopped. Most mornings this trip the rain has kept us inside and hoping, kept us inside as a powerful storm moved down from the mid-Atlantic and swathed the eastern half of the country in heavy clouds, cool air and rain, plenty of rain for three days in a row. Only this morning after the last bucket-washer of the night passed (it drummed its flamenco on the tin roof for hours) and the blue sky swept in, in patches, from the Caribbean, only this morning have we been able to see anything.

Barred antshrikes sound in the backwoods—a classic jungle call from a small, unassuming bird, like a tropical robin belting out the note to the international rainforest anthem. We stumble (we're up before staff has made the coffee) through the lodge's gardens. The tall sway of coconut palms. Heliconia and wild plantain. A hedge of sea grape along the beach behind which the surf pounds and roars. A flash of yellow in the wisteria. We set the scope and there it is, a prothonotary warbler, bright gold with steel-blue wings and a striking black eye, forging deliberately, using its long bill like tweezers to pull insects from the crevassed bark.

This is a new bird for me. I mark it in the book, look up at Luis and ask, "Did you know that this bird is named for the Vatican clerks who were lucky enough, maybe rich enough, to wear golden hoods?"

"Really?"

"That's what prothonotary means."

"You know I always wonder what that word mean."

"When I left you, I was but the learner. Now I am the master," I say in my deepest Darth Vader voice. Luis looks at me funny, folds the scope's tripod back up, and walks off shouldering it.

I am thrilled to have taught Luis something—it is almost always the other way around—but the fact is, since we had been shoved inside by the rain for so long, I was bored and went wandering the Internet on the lodge's computer. I looked up birds of the Caribbean and just happened to read about the prothonotary warbler the night before. The bird is also weirdly famous for establishing a connection between Alger Hiss and Whittaker Chambers. In testimony before the House Un-American Activities Committee, Chambers, the once and former communist turned witness and name-namer, testified that Hiss was an enthusiastic birdwatcher who bragged once about seeing a prothonotary warbler. When Hiss later testified to the same detail—the same small, golden-hooded bird—

many on the committee became convinced of their friendship and Hiss's guilt.

I don't say anything about that.

§

In the 21ˢᵗ century, in our contemporary-technological culture, in this age of irony, we distrust the traditional reunion with nature as a means of solace. I write these thoughts as the rain pummels the lodge and then collects in huge puddles lining the wooden walkways. As the wind rushes in from the east and tosses the tress around. *Our current intellectual position demands that we refuse consolation from the natural world. Nature exists separately from us, the argument goes; we can only know it distantly and inconsequentially and it certainly does not join us in our grief. To suggest otherwise is to risk foolishness and a kind of adolescent bathos.* And yeah, that's all true, but like all of my thinking here, it feels like things are far more complicated than that.

The natural world does not exist, of course, only in the imagination, only in the representation of its human observers. That kind of solipsism is reductive and ultimately useless. There is a fragile world alive and thriving beyond the walls of culture and safety and technology we have built to protect and coddle ourselves. It is alive and we are distant from it, as our very words tell us, and thus we must work a mental two-step and let the landscape be both imagined and real at the same time. To hold both, contradictory ideas at the same time alive and buzzing in the hive of our thoughts. That's negative capability. That's what John Keats says, too, in his nightingale poem:

> I cannot see what flowers are at my feet,
>   Nor what soft incense hangs upon the boughs,
> But, in embalmed darkness, guess each sweet
>   Wherewith the seasonable month endows
> The grass, the thicket, and the fruit-tree wild;
> White hawthorn, and the pastoral eglantine;
>   Fast fading violets cover'd up in leaves;

> *And mid-May's eldest child,*
> *The coming musk-rose, full of dewy wine,*
> *The murmurous haunt of flies on summer*
> *eves.*

The real world, the physical world, is hard to see. We look on in error and with the limits of our time and mind. We cannot see the flowers at our feet. But in the imagined realm of the pastoral, in the poetic world that echoes the song of the nightingale, Keats can at least guess at and create a word that follows the form of the natural world. He imagines a world so like ours, but one made of flies and musk roses, made of the fast-fade of violets and words, words that resemble that very physical world he cannot fully see.

Just so, my quetzal, my pelicans, my colonies of leaf-cutter ants tunneling through vast, glowing cities of their own design: they are all part my own creation—a formation of desire and memory—and part their own being, autonomous and alive. The bright, startling form of the quetzal, that green and vermillion phantasm posed in an almond tree, is for me the emblem of that particular mountain landscape, the Savegre River valley that descends from the heights of *Cerro de la Muerte* and out to the welcoming, Pacific lowlands. Likewise, the aerial prowess of brown pelicans will in many ways define my understanding of that particular stretch of rainforest beach on the Corcovado Peninsula. The pelicans live on in the imagination because I am long gone from Costa Rica and in memory the mind is most powerful. The quetzal's vibrant life is a locus of desire and loss and I write it into existence from a far distance.

§

The prothonotary warbler dips its head and makes a *tseip, tseip* call, and spins off into the higher trees near the river.

"That's gotta be new for you," Luis says. "Rare to see on this slope."

"Yup. 391. We're getting there."

"Good. Let's keep going. This is good morning. Lots of these guys they come out to dry off after all the rain."

We keep walking, skirting the huge, leaf-filled puddles and deadfall from the storm. Twisting our necks, stopping at every birdcall. The sunlight is just beginning to march down the tops of the tallest trees as the sun rises over the horizon. In the sea grape, near the ocean, we can see the tremble of something. A small flutter, then a pause.

"That's a warbler. Some kind. Can't see this guy." Luis drops the legs of the scope and trains it on the tuft of leaves this bird has staked out.

"Gray with yellow. Definitely a warbler. Bright wing bars, bit of gold on the back. Strong striped face."

I look. I can see the bird, but at this distance, even with my binoculars, even when I get a turn at the scope, I am struggling to keep up with Luis' description. I can see the bird and it is gray-gold. I can even see the face striping, a bit, I think. But it won't hold still and the scope's frame is small. It hops and flits from branch to branch, evading my eye. We pull out the book and wade into the warbler section. There are sixty-eight warblers and gnat-catchers resident in Costa Rica ranging from the obvious (the black-throated blue) to the minute variations that cover the rest of the plate—magnolia, mangrove, mourning— variations so small that my response to warblers is often to simply give up.

"No, no, no." Luis is ticking off the birds our hopping friend is not. "This guy have more gray in him. Not the yellow. Not the hooded. Canada? No. Not him either. Still more gray."

We flip the pages back and forth. Luis checks the scope again. The bird's still there, but framed in the new light of the day, the milk-white sun coming through the low, thin clouds above the ocean, he's hard to see.

"Blue-winged? No. Too yellow. Has to be this guy. Golden-winged warbler. Yes." He checks the scope again. "Yes. I am sure of it. Check the book."

I read, out loud: *fairly common fall migrant, uncommon but widespread winter resident on Caribbean lowlands.* "Gotta be him." But then I read the note under the blue-winged warbler: *hybridizes frequently with blue-winged warbler…which resembles the golden-wing but with the face pattern of the blue-wing.* Maybe it's not him. Maybe it's a hybrid or the blue wing. I trust Luis, but I can't tell. There are too many possibilities.

I say nothing. And mark the golden-winged in my book with a notation: Tortuguero, 2010.

§

At the Wilson Botanical Station near Las Cruces, Costa Rica, there is a garden of spectacular tropical plants from around the world. The garden falls away from the oddly luxuriant science station that looms above it like the lit prow of a huge ship. A few cabins gather around the lodge in green-roofed anonymity. The terraced gardens and succulent plants and flowers flow down the hillsides and into the paths of crushed stone that curl around the property like tendrils.

Out walking the paths in the soft welcome of early evening, in the wet fronds of a leather banana, I find an emerald glass frog: small, but gangly, with egg-speckled skin (a deep emerald, naturally) and long toes like gelled drops of water. I locate this very territorial frog by his call, a loud, sharp *dink* like a cheap wine glass rapped with a spoon. This one's a male; the turquoise spines of its forelegs used to grasp and hold the female give it away. Many species of frog congregate here, encouraged by the sprinklers that nightly wash over the gardens. The night air is filled with frogs claiming their territories. One call resembles a cell phone in the distance, while another sounds like a weightlifter grunting. Others chirp or twitter, songbirds for the dark hours.

§

Luis and I move out of the scrub, the sea grape and the gavilán, beyond the lone monkey pot tree, out onto the wild and swept beach. It runs miles north and south and is almost always empty of human life. The surf is rough—strong rip currents pull swimmers down and bull sharks and crocodiles patrol these waters. No one swims here. The lodges all face the river and the canals and turn their backs on the sea. The sun has pulled above the eastern clouds building up over the Caribbean and the light hits the trees behind us the way the wind hits us now, fresh and strong and clean as a new day. Sanderlings run the surf line in packs, their tiny legs spinning and sprinting to follow the arc of each wave as it recedes into the billowing surf. A pack of yellowlegs stands with heads into the wind, waiting, and among them a whimbrel, a bit darker, but still with that brown mottle of the shore bird's camouflage, and a bit larger, too. But what really gives it away is the huge curving bill, like a scythe. Beyond the surf, royal and common terns dive for fish, bright as knives in the clean light. Their bills burning orange. There is nothing new here. I had all these birds marked in my book long ago.

My list climbed rapidly to more than 300 in the first several years—the big names ticked off quickly: scarlet macaw, keel-billed toucan, blue-crowned motmot, violet saber-wing. These are the birds that most people come to the tropics to see—the exotic, the flamboyant, the unmistakable. I have loved and still love seeing them; I love showing them to students and to others. When my son was eight and Jennifer and I took him out of school and brought him down to spend one February in Costa Rica, we went out looking for the resplendent quetzal in the cloud forest, and we found him in the twisted mist and strangler figs, sitting stoic on a horizontal branch and filling the afternoon with his whistling call—*chirr roop, chirr roop*. His red chest blazed against the mottle of multiple greens that make up the cloud forest: all that leaf and moss and lichen and fern. When Julian had to write a report for his teacher about what he learned and saw, one of the main things he highlighted and drew was the quetzal—blocky and bright and big on the page with words scrawled under it: *we saw the Qasall not maney people have seen it.*

To my students, seeing a toucan flying in the late light, with its enormous bill almost completely balancing its thin body, justifies the trip down. They want the *rainforest*, the exotic, the wild. They often stand open-mouthed at first, literally dumbstruck, when they first see the flocks of scarlet macaws that scavenge the coast of the Osa Peninsula for wild avocados and figs, the vermillion ruckus of them filling up the sky. To see one, maybe two, that's what they expect, if they are lucky. They never expect to see a flock of forty chattering scarlet and cobalt birds squawking through the air. (*Unmistakable*, says the guidebook.) They never expect to stand beneath a wild avocado decorated like a Christmas tree with a whole, rowdy flock of scarlet macaws.

§

Here in my journals, in the words I write at night while sitting at the bar before dinner like a tropical Gatsby gazing across the water at that green future he could almost but never quite touch, with the width of the river before me dark and fluid and striped with lights from the docks on the opposite shore, I am trying to gather together two inseparable and divided kingdoms: the world and the word. I am trying to understand my own complicated, messy thinking about the natural world. So I probably need to deal more directly with the fact that there are two kinds of landscapes: the external landscape we see and experience and the interior landscape, a projection of the exterior landscape onto the screen of consciousness. The exterior is fact and thing, oak and mist and quetzal, the small swerve of the river descending into the valley. The interior is impression and imprint, idea and conception. It is the word. The two landscapes are separate, interdependent and fundamentally connected. In one word, or one name—*Las Cruces* or *Tortuguero* or even *home*—so much lives in that one word that it cannot be a physical thing alone. The word *Las Cruces* carries a deep, terraced garden bathed in the perpetual springtime of those sprinklers, the infinite regression into a tiny ecosystem choked with living frogs. *Tortuguero* carries rivers and rain and turtles, birds and clouds and the wet heat of midday. And *home*? Home depends, doesn't it, on the reader and the wealth of her imagined life that lives alone inside her skull. I believe our minds are defined by the particular landscapes they occupy, just as much as they are by the DNA that builds them. If that's true, then, despite our desire, we cannot separate our world from our language of that world. If words seem limiting, if names corral beings into tiny spaces too small for them to fit, that is only half of the illusion of language. Language, words, they carry space within them. They are caverns of great size carried in small packages of sound. They limit in limitless ways.

On the other hand, birdwatching and listing are at the heart of many assumptions I am making about the natural world—a world both highly complex and distant and yet intimately familiar. Listing birds, keeping track of species, defining, delineating. These are the tools of the rational mind. Counting is a means of control; it is a variation on science and naming (the Adamic principle): the desire to know through organization and system. Birdwatching is a variation on the system of Linnaean taxonomy itself—kingdom, phylum, class, order, family, genus, species—with the understanding of evolution that exists within it (speciation is evolution and vice versa). And counting lies at the heart of birding. The pursuit of birds becomes in some way a mirror that shows us how we see the world. Birds become knowledge and they become control. The idea that there are 9,500 avian species in the world (or 900 in Costa Rica for that matter) is only a rough estimate, especially since the scientific understanding of what and is and is not a species keeps changing. Generally speaking, a species is any group of organisms capable of reproducing and producing viable offspring, but where to draw that line in real life, in individual cases, is often very difficult and subject to revision and complication. So what does it mean to see one-third or one-half of all the species in Costa Rica? Such numbers are estimates at the edge of nothing, or everything. Such gestures are akin to holding up a thousand glasses of seawater and saying, *I have seen the ocean.*

The very idea that I can name something here, on this page; not here where I am on a barrier island in Costa Rica, surrounded by this flamboyance of birds and the ruckus of the garden, but on a page, and have you recognize it and reproduce it in your own mind is laughable. And yet it works. Every. Damn. Day. Our language and our intelligence have gathered their fruits from the very same garden, the pastoral garden we have made from the world. The evolution of our language and of our intelligence itself (to my mind, one is defined by the other) is a basic result of an interaction between the mind (in the act of creating metaphor) and the natural world and it follows the pattern of life itself: a limited number of building blocks that together allow for a system of almost infinite complexity and wonder.

The infinite possibilities of language and metaphor are, as I have said, the mirrors of the infinite possibilities of DNA. Our genetic life starts with four basic building blocks—nucleotides, that is, the subunits of DNA made from four nucleobases: guanine, adenine, thymine, and cytosine—and from that tiny sample an impossible wealth of life erupts in its multitudinous forms. Likewise, our language, with a limited storehouse of sounds (44 phonemes in English) conjures a complexity matched only by organic life. The world affects the word and the word the world. They are created out of conflict and contamination. Each damages and heals the other. The possibilities of the word are defined by the possibilities of the world and the power of the world circumscribed by the language we use to define and contain it. Our minds, it seems, don't accept that we are separate and isolate, despite our 21ˢᵗ-century distance. Despite our irony. Despite mine. Our words—when we speak about our deepest selves, as we do in poetry—need to reach out and find their equivalence in the natural world.

§

With soft, wet hands, I pull the emerald frog from the long wet leaf. He comes off gummy, the pads of his toes hanging on and stretching. Beneath a deep green back, his abdomen is glossy white, translucent really, and beneath my flashlight his heart beats, terrified. I see, through his glass skin, the inside of a living body, and watch the tempo of his pulse and the gluey movement of lungs. His tiny heart pulses, quick as a bird's. Blood flushes through his veins. His stomach works on the jammy marsh of insects that made up his last meal as his intestines snake and undulate against themselves like dark rivers. Arteries and veins divide and subdivide in iterations, the architecture of a ruddy forest. Through the lucent skin, through the window of another creature's body, a world opens, becomes wetland, becomes rainforest, becomes valley, and, as fragile as it is, becomes beautiful.

§

These days I want the new bird, the small bird, the hard to identify bird, the mysterious little chirper in the underbrush that I can't quite find. I want the challenge, the novelty, the new number—but of course that leads me to the crux of the matter. Intent. Why am I dragging

116

myself from bed in the early hours of dawn to slop around with a heavy book and binoculars? What's the reason for this search? Do I want to see birds (if so, they are all around me—Tortuguero is particularly lush with avian life) or do I simply want to run up the score? Increase my list? Is the count more important than the bird? Did I give up on wonder and beauty? When did that happen?

My list is based on an arbitrary set of rules—my own personal game that I am playing in the natural world—but the rules feel no less important and valid for that. The birds have to be in the guidebook and I have to see them in Costa Rica. (Many species, obviously, migrate and I could find a number of them in the US, but that would be breaking the rules.) I have to see the bird; hearing its song is not enough and I have to be sure of the sighting. Sometimes, as I count up toward 400, birding can feel less like appreciation and more like hoarding, like I am stacking up the numbers in some impossible quest to be good enough, to see more. At times, climbing out of bed before the sun is up to tromp around in a DEET-soaked sweat feels like a job. But at other times, I stand stunned and happy in the face of some new kind of avian grace: the small, hard buzz of a magnificent hummingbird, the cobalt thrill of a blue dacnis, a great flock of black-bellied whistling-ducks, honking from the wetlands of Palo Verde and blackening the dark and wind-ruffled water of *Río Tempisque* as it flows through the buff and dust of the leafless, tropical dry forest, thousands of ducks taking off in one thunder of wings.

Back on the beach, with a fresh wind blowing in hard from the east and the sun climbing its ladder into the sky, Luis finds a king vulture in the dead limbs of a far distant "flame of the forest," or bastard teak tree. A huge bird—through the scope, we can see its startling white shoulder and crimson head—its wingspan can reach 2 meters. As we watch, it drops from the tree and grabs the warming air with its enormous wings. It pushes out and up into the sky, carving turns in the scattered blue and broken clouds of morning. Luis says, with a kind of quiet pride, "Very rare we see that bird, very rare."

VIII.

In the upper reaches of the Amazon watershed, there lives a species of bee that will strip every hair from your head instead of swelling your body with venom, a bee that will leave you bald and clean and strangely unstung. At least that is what I have been told. Whether these bees and their hive, cylindrical and birchy, like a log hanging from the tips of the thin branches at the edge of a fig tree's reach, actually exist, almost doesn't matter. Because of that story, their hive makes in my mind the shape of threat that hangs above the white river south of Iquitos in the meandering fan of the Tahuayo River. Whether these bees and their hive houses such an amazing hazard doesn't really matter much on the page; I could lie and make it true. Who's to know, really? The world's full of marvels. And yet it does matter. The fact is this was never about the bees, really, or the fig tree. It is about the weight the story carries, the heaviness of a narrative that always returns to the speaking self—told by our guide in the boat as we thrum upriver toward the Tahuayo Lodge. It is about the strange menace of power inside that story and then in my mind where it hums and thrives. It is about the transfer of that power from me to you, like the sudden shock of static electricity. It is the sense of threat hanging above the world that leaves you stripped to flushed flesh beneath gaudy palms that tick above you in the wind.

It feels to me that one of the purposes of story and myth is to shape the relationship between the twin aspects of land: the interior and exterior landscapes. Myth and story form an essential relationship to where we live, how we live, and why. What we say about our world defines our relationship with that world and, further, story repairs—it returns the listener to a primordial relationship with the land, or so the theory goes. If we say the right words, think the right thoughts, we can heal the damage we have done to the world. That's the idea. Through story, we can reorder our confusion and realign our thoughts in new and healthy ways. The assumption that story can reorder consciousness, however, seems to assume that such a reordering will always be for the benefit of the individual and the world. In other words, the reordered state granted through story will be a healthy one. The land, engaged this way, will clarify our psychological confusion and bring us closer to a kind of truth. But what if the paradox and inherent contradiction that are inherent in myth and story, instead, turn us away from the world? What if our stories are likewise in opposition to the ordering of consciousness, and they push us away from the land?

In many stories from the western tradition, the ones I teach back in the states when I start my course on writing about place, home defines our sense of character. Where home lives there lives identity. Or its opposite. Home is what Achilles gives up to gain the perfection of glory after ten drifting years battling through Asia. Home is what Moses loses in the desert in a moment of faithlessness, in the broken promises of his followers, and what Cain loses in the rage of a favorite son abandoned for his brother. Home is what Huck Finn quits as he lights out for the territory ahead of all the rest.

Sitting here in the Tahuayo Lodge, with this Amazon tributary shining beneath the night's onyx light and the air carrying whispers of rain, I imagine Moses in the desert on Pisgah, forty long years after his glory days in Egypt, with the tents of the people of the Lord lit up like lanterns below him. He has been talking to God, listening to the stories that he will write on rolls of animal parchment. He has also been told that the green-gone-gold valley beyond the dark hills and deep river is not for him. *Get thee up into the top of Pisgah*, says the Lord, *and lift up thine eyes westward, and northward, and southward, and eastward, and behold it with thine eyes: for thou shalt not go over this Jordan.* Because his followers mutter in their tents, cursing perhaps their exile (*the 38th year of it!*), Moses has been condemned to a permanent trek—he has an appointment with the jackals and the vultures, to use Bruce Chatwin's phrase. He has been told the story of Cain, told the story of that rage and violence, the blade crashing down through the skull, told the story of a son who has lost the favor of his father. In these moments, Moses must think of him. Cain the wanderer. Cain the outcast. Moses must see him almost formed, his dark shape marked by the hand of God, must see him just beyond the firelight, beckoning.

It appears to be no accident that Abel is Yahweh's chosen one. He is the goatherd, shepherd of the earliest pastoral, wandering child of a god who seems to love nothing more than a good road trip. It is Yahweh who leads people out of cities—Abraham from Babylon, the Jews from Egypt, his own son into the desert to face the temptation of the adversary. Cain, the farmer, the tender of the land, is exiled from the favor of God. It is as if his very connection to place puts him on the wrong side of God's chosen people. That Cain's punishment is to wander the Earth—protected from revenge by the hand of God—suggests a strange reciprocity; Cain has taken Abel's place, become the trekking loner beloved in part because of his wandering. That's what the American in me finds in this story; Yahweh has transformed Cain and made of him what he most desires in us.

§

In the mornings when I am out slopping around in the rainforest muck looking, always looking, for birds, I recognize the risk of reducing nature to charismatic megafauna and moments of pure wonder. The quetzal may symbolize the cloud forest, the scarlet macaw the lowland tropics (and, yes, the world would be very much poorer without their presence), but how much less valuable is the riverside wren, a bird I have often heard but never seen (its *victory, victory, victory* call filling up small stream-cut valleys across the Caribbean slope), its tiny shape flitting just out of eyesight in the scrub? My Costa Rican numbers represent more than the charismatic; they represent the small and the quotidian (the clay-colored robin, the rufous-collared sparrow) and they represent diversity—almost 400 of the 900 different shades of avian life that Costa Rica holds inside its cloak. Luis, who has lived his whole life in the country, and spent much of that life tromping through the woods looking for animals, hunting them in different ways, has marked more than 700 birds in his book—even more torn and battered than mine— and it is unlikely I will ever come close to him.

§

In another vision from a very different tradition—one of my all-time favorites—Achilles reclines in his tent. The body of Hector, man-killing Hector, still golden and unmarked in spite of Achilles' best efforts to defile the corpse, remains hooked to his chariot with thongs of raw leather. Priam enters, disguised by the will of the gods. They talk. They drink. They weep. Priam for his son and his doomed city. Achilles for his own father, abandoned, whom he will never see again in this world. Achilles long ago made his choice to live for his future glory, not his present, local life, but he gives the body back. He violates the code of the hero. In this closing moment of pity and deeply human feeling, does he give Hector's body back to Priam because he finally understands the full, terrifying nature of his choice? Does he understand that he has given up his domestic tranquility and wishes to offer Priam one last, fragile bit of what he cannot have? He knows now that he will have spent the last years of his life chasing the retreating ramparts of Troy, sleeping in his ship. He has abandoned the light-wet hearth and gentle ease of Phthia. His habitat is his grave of everlasting glory. His loss is his hearth and home.

§

Luis and I have driven the students up into the *Cordillera de Talamanca* for the last few days before we have to descend back to San José and the flight home. The end of another course. My last chance to cross 400. Today, on our hike, which began on top of *Cerro de la Muerte*, we've crossed through four major eco-systems—starting with the high, alpine *páramo* where the dwarf bamboo and alpine irises cover the hillside and the low chusquea shrubs hunker down to shield themselves from the constant winds, where volcano hummingbirds zip and spin around the edges of our vision. Tiny, these birds measure only 7.5 centimeters from beak to tail with bronze-green upper parts and rufous-edged black outer tail feathers. The throat grey-purple. The other primary birds up here are mountain robins and clay-colored robins (both, in fact, thrushes). The clay-colored robin is a plain brown bird with a musical song and flight-call like that of the American robin, but harsher and more grating. In Costa Rica it is known as the *yigüirro* and, somehow, most likely because it likes to live near human habitation, it has been named the Costa Rican national bird, which disgusts Luis and aggravates him to no end.

"Ugly bird," he says. "Ugly."

§

In Dante's version, Ulysses even gives up Ithaca after he has tried so hard and long to turn his ship toward home. Condemned for his trickery and guile in building the horse that brought down the great city of Troy (a palace of the domestic and the local when compared to its enemies, the wandering Greeks) and encased within a living flame in Hades, Ulysses speaks to Dante and relates to Dante what he told his crew:

> *My brothers, I said, you who have now reached the West...*
> *Don't reject, in the small time we have left, the experience*
> *Of that uninhabited world that lies behind the sunset.*

What Dante knows—exile that he was—is the paradox of the domestic. *Home* is at once the nearly unreachable island of Ithaca, where Penelope haunts her loom, the unattainable land of milk and honey, a place worth 40 years in the desert scraping manna off the sunbaked stones to get back to, and at the same time, a fundamentally unfulfilling address, a world the direct opposite of glory, wisdom, and virtue. Why? What is

124

there about the local that both compels us and drives us away? How can Dante's Ulysses (who is clearly a version of Dante himself) believe that the life he so desired, cast away on Circe's island, has become base and the antithesis of nobility? Why does Yahweh favor the traveler at the expense of the settler? Why is the fundamental structure of our myth, from the Greco-Roman through the Judeo-Christian and into our own time (think Johnny Appleseed, Huck Finn, Jack Kerouac), based on the premise that staying put is the equivalent of self-destruction and that wandering brings health, dignity, freedom, glory, and intellectual engagement? I think this tension is something inborn in us, born in the long savannas of the African bush, something that pushes us out away from comfort and demands that we put heel to toe to abandon home for the gauzy horizon. This is the American in us. This is the nomad in us, the wanderer. It is the drifter and migrant in us, the traveller. But it is also the poet.

What Dante tells us here is that the goal of the biological and poetic self is to proceed in ignorance, to forever enter new lands of meaning, different landscapes—both physically and of the imagination. If the landscape is to grant us health and knowledge it must be refreshed and strange before us, wonderful in its newness. In many ways it is safety and comfort that grates; the comfortable world, to my mind, is the stagnant world. Life is lived best pushing at the edges. If this is true, then the project of my life becomes a continual turn toward the source; a refusal of home, comfort, and the status quo. I must step out anew each time and move into a landscape that is as cleared of names and language as I can manage; I must walk out into the desert in ignorance and rethink and reclaim my place in the world.

§

The students and I started early at top of *Cerro de la Muerte,* in a cold mist blowing through the chusquea, a rough grass-like plant in the bamboo family. I know this place. The ghostly, moon-colored mist that gallops across this peak. The deep emptiness we walk into as though crossing an English moor on top of a tropical mountain, dropping down down, always down with the light building beneath us and the bamboo growing taller and rising above our heads and then falling away as stunted oak and cypress take over. The transition happens quickly and suddenly we realize that a new type of forest has risen up, a quiet forest of mist and twisted oak limbs covered with a froth of moss and lichen. Birdsong absent. Occasionally I hear the high pitched twittering of a fiery-throated hummingbird overhead and catch a quick glimpse of the small dark bird but miss the brilliance of its blue cap or the sunburst throat that it shows, in the right light, when it perches. As we drop farther down the trail with the deep, blurry *c'cooo c'cooos* of the flocking band-tailed pigeons haunting the distance, the oaks grow larger and larger until they tower up around us in pillars. Huge trees, massive, with buttress roots we can stand between. Here and there patches of forest where the trees are covered with a blonde moss that hangs from each branch, a moss that in the sunlight, in the rare sunlight that breaks through the clouds, turns the trees to something from a fairy tale: a forest of spun gold.

§

Solvitur ambulando. It is solved by walking. This is the 4th century B.C.; Greek philosopher Diogenes's phrase. And I repeat it kilometer after kilometer as I descend down the forever hillside of *Cerro de la Muerte.* I drop down through the rough grasslands and fields of wild iris, blue and tough as leather in the cold wind, down through stunted trees growing taller and taller, down through groves of oak draped in cloaks of golden moss that turn the forest to splendor when the sun breaks through the clouds. I walk and I walk. Out into the world, and down toward the lodge. But what if what is solved by walking is really only my selfish desire for novelty? What if the choice I have made is Achilles' choice, really, the refusal of the local and the real and the domestic to seek out an imagined glory beyond death? I fear death and thus I consume as Achilles consumed glory and it consumed him. Now, some people consume products, but I am consuming landscapes, often artificial and sentimentalized versions of landscapes. My consumption is defined by cultural exploration. Exploration is a kind of Troy, the fabled city that lies just outside our grasp. But I fail to see that, as it was *not* for Moses, the land of milk and honey isn't mine. It will never be, because I have told myself the wrong stories. Like Achilles, I am outcast by my own desire and may just wind up wandering endlessly in a desert campaign of my own creation.

The story of Moses tells me that I will look for a home but never find it. Cain's story suggests that God's love goes to the wanderer. The story of Achilles tells me that I will never find a home because I have chosen to abandon the one I have; I have given up the sheltered hearth for the open road. The term hearth here denotes not simply the constructed domestic of the domicile, but the "holy space" at the center of the self's experience in the world. All these stories tell us (tell me) that we are, by definition, outcast from the world we would choose. From home. And that we will almost always make the choice to pursue that imagined perfection beyond the horizon. But what if such perfection exists only in the mind, in the structure of image and language that defines it? Does this argument mean that we will be forever unable to find any kind of permanent, domestic peace? That we are forever tied to the Huck Finns of our nature, continuously lighting out for the territory ahead of everyone else? And what happens to us when we run out of territory to light out into?

§

By afternoon the students and I have made it down into the cloud forest above the lodge; we are tired and spent, our knees aching from the hours of descent. Tree ferns and epiphytes, bromeliads and curtains of hanging moss, with the sun still splintering through the broken clouds. We slop through the many streams that cascade down from the mountains above and turn the trail to mud. Glorious.

I am trailing the group, as I usually do, sweeping to make sure no stragglers get left behind, Luis in the lead, when I hear a hard scolding *kew kew kew* from the underbrush—a shaggy, moss-hung lip of the trail that appears wall-like against the light of the sun. The students and Luis are far ahead. I am alone on the trail. I pause and listen and there it is again, that wren-like scold, hard and fast. I can hear where the bird is calling from but I can see almost nothing against the thickness of the scrub. Then movement in a low gap in the bamboo not 10 feet off the trail, a small dark bird kicking up leaf litter, looking for insects on the forest floor. Without my binoculars (even at 10 feet) I can see little, the shade too dark, the bird too small. But with my field glasses I see the bird clearly, now that I know where to look—very dark rufous and black with a strong white eyebrow. Very distinctive, but I have no idea what he might be. He's completely new for me and Luis is far ahead. I am on my own to figure him out. He's not in the small bird book I carry with me when I hike (the full guide's too heavy for a full-day slog), so I try to hold on to the image of the bird in my mind as I finish the hike. I think, *wren-like, small and dark with that strong white brow.* And I repeat this mantra down the trail to the main road, but by the time I am back to the lodge I've lost it and I am thinking about new things—the color of the peaches (small balls of dawn) in the orchard above the lodge, the spiral of a red-tailed hawk in the sky above the valley, the precision in a hummingbird's nest in a small *Cecropia* by the side of the road.

§

I wonder whether we can, in fact, grow to know and love a place, a specific place, with all the tenacity and merit it deserves. I am certain that people often love the landscapes they find themselves in. I feel that way, clearly. But what if we love an idealized landscape that no longer exists (if indeed it ever did)? We believe in places abstracted from experience and only tenuously connected to the real and tangible earth. Both out of ignorance (which is not, let's be clear, stupidity) and divergent aspirations. Our new stories have absorbed the conflicting desires we posses regarding place—the desire for both novelty and familiarity—but they also contain the seeds of what we once knew. This landscape we name as ours and believe in is an imagined creation of myth and story fed by powerful commercial forces eager to exploit us through national marketing and advertising campaigns.

Let me give you an example. Maybe you have seen this one: Three or four intrepid hikers slash through the rainforest. Dressed in sweated-through, khaki adventure shirts, shorts, and boots as the rich foliage lunges at them, they are clearly far from civilization. One man, his hair matted and sweaty with work, pats down his pockets and says, somewhat incongruously, "I lost my credit card back there." The guide, a young man, unshaven and with a world-traveler-look about him, reassures him, "Well don't worry. There's nobody around for miles."

Cut to the next scene: a hut that combines every Tarzan fantasy with an updated, ecotourism motif. Up on stilts in the rain forest, the hut is filled with monkeys and apes enjoying the spoils of the modern capitalist world—CD players playing funk (we'll try to ignore the racist overtones of this), a big screen TV, computers, and even a disco ball—all purchased fraudulently with the man's Capital One credit card. They frolic and flirt with the camera and one another. Involved in the festivities are white-faced capuchins, chimpanzees, and orangutans.

What's the problem here? There are a number, but for my interests it is the wildlife. Why put these three animals together? Because as any decent wildlife biologist will tell you, they represent species from three different continents. White-faced capuchins (*Cebus capucinus*) are new world monkeys who roam the tropics of Central and South America. Chimpanzees (either *Pan troglodytes,* the common chimp, or *Pan paniscus,* the pygmy chimpanzee) occupy the forests of West and Central Africa. Orangutans (*Pongo pygmaeus*) are solitary climbers who inhabit a variety of forest ecosystems on the islands of Sumatra and Borneo located south of the Malay Peninsula. Obviously there is no one patch of rainforest in the world (outside of the mind of Madison Avenue) where all these apes and monkeys might conceivably interact.

It's a fantasy, so why does this matter? It matters because this ignorance is part of a larger system of natural or geographic illiteracy—the willful unknowing of place, a tendency that is, perhaps, tied to our impulse to wander, our condition as nomads and vagabonds. It is quite clear that the creators of this ad have no *real place* in mind where the action takes place. It exists in the mental and sentimental, a realm created for easy consumption and based on hundreds of years of images and stories, from *The Heart of Darkness* to Tarzan. In fact, this place only exists as a *word,* that one collection of sound and sense we call "Jungle." This imagined landscape is populated likewise by the broad category of "Monkeys." Specific species are irrelevant, geographical incongruities immaterial.

§

It is only when I get to my room and pull the mudded boots from my feet, when I've stood beneath the hot blast of the shower and am finally sitting on the small porch in front of my room watching the hummingbirds flash around the garden, watching the slow slide of light leaving the canyon and wondering just how long I need to wait before I can go get a beer at the bar, only then do I remember. I grab the book and start leafing through the plates. Obviously a ground bird, so that's where I start, with the antbirds and the furnariids. Nothing. The black-headed ant thrush is dark like my guy but too big and no white eyebrow. Plus he lives on the Caribbean slope and we're on the Pacific now—ground birds don't cross these mountains very well. The immaculate antbird? He's middle elevation and the right dark coloring. But that guy (as Luis would say) has a blue eye ring that runs to the bill. Can't be him. Next page—*Antwrens, Spinetails and Other Small Understory Birds*—and there he is. Easy. The dark gray fading to rufous along the tail, the strong white brow. Highlands. It all fits. Silvery-fronted tapaculo. I read:

> *…skulks in dense undergrowth of highland forest, especially thickets and bamboo tangles along streams and ravines, so inconspicuous and secretive it would be considered very rare were it not for its loud, distinctive calls.*

Exactly what I saw and heard. I mark him and make a note in the book—Savegre 2010, Las Robles trail—and move on. But something about this guy sticks with me. Part of it was that I had to work to see him and make the ID. Part of it is that phrase, *so inconspicuous and secretive it would be considered very rare.* I am always pleased to find a rare bird and discouraged when I make a new sighting only to read in the guide that this new bird is "common to such and such a locale." When I tell Luis later, he looks at me with a kind of astonishment.

"You saw this guy? For sure?"

"Yep, absolutely. The eyebrow, and that call, gives him away."

"That's a good sighting, *profe*. What number is that?"

"399."

§

In the film *Maverick*, from a few years back, Mel Gibson plays a gambler struggling to reach the big game on a riverboat on the Missouri, somewhere in Eastern Montana, but the director, Richard Donner, seems to have no idea where the Missouri River is geographically, or worse yet doesn't care. Gibson travels from the bare-bones wash of the Sonoran desert through an area that might be the Four Corners region to what is clearly the Valley of the Yosemite, in California, all the while ostensibly traveling *Northeast* to Montana to a riverboat on the Missouri. Notwithstanding the fact that these trips of weeks or months by horseback are compressed into a few days journey, these locales make little or no geographic sense. They make sense only in, again, a kind of mental and linguistic category—this time the category of the word: *West*. The categorical *West* exists in a perpetual wash of images—Ansel Adams's photographs of Yosemite, Georgia O'Keefe's portraits of New Mexico, every badlands western and ski-town film ever made. What this film gives us is a re-encapsulation of the *West*, packaged for easy consumption and tied up with the beautiful faces of Mel Gibson and Jodie Foster.

It happens again and again. When Thelma and Louise race through the southeast toward New Mexico before heading south for Mexico (it was important that they skirt Texas, if you remember), they wind up, inexplicably, at the Grand Canyon. The women begin in an industrial (masculine) landscape populated by oil derricks and trucks and they flee west, into the free space of American identity; the masculine landscape of the opening scenes is replaced by more natural (read: feminine) geography. But, landscape and place here attains the status of backdrop, used to foster the easily digested and clearly articulated language of the American self. It's irrelevant, again, *where* we are in reality and *where* that geography is in relationship to other places. What matters is the image, the *characterization* and *sentimentalization* of nature and landscape. We create these unreal and simplified landscapes so that they are available for marketing and consumption. This loss of specificity and complexity happens so dependably in our culture and with such repetition that it becomes in a sense pathological.

And I am guilty as well. I simplify landscape. I synthesize and combine. I have done so here, even as I rail against it. Turning ten trips to Costa Rica and one to Peru into an attempt at a unified whole. And worse. Remember that cathedral with *el Señor de los Temblores, with* Christ as the Lord of Earthquakes? That guy, as Luis would say, he lives in Cuzco, Peru, not San José, Costa Rica. And remember those wasps? That hive full of wasps that swam out from the deadfall to pincushion my face and neck and back with toxin? Yeah, those wasps. Well all that happened in Peru, too, not Costa Rica, as I led you to believe. Altering the timeline and falsifying place made my narrative better. It unified the story and brought the arc of the first act of this little performance to a dramatic close. Christ taking in the pain of the world and controlling it, mastering it with his suffering. The curtain rushing down on me as I wandered like Lear through the ever-twilight of that old growth forest shivering and wondering if my throat would close. I put scenes separated by years and by thousands of miles—similar landscapes, sure, but similar is not same—I put them together because it suited the purpose of my story better. That's my excuse, but it's a weak one. Forgive me if you will.

§

I left Costa Rica in January, with my list still at 399. It sits there still. It may not be until years later that I can cross the threshold and start working toward 450 (half of all the birds in Costa Rica—now *that* seems like a worthwhile goal). But I don't want to leave the narrative there—it feels wrong, unfinished. So I will add one more piece, one more story that might allow this all to make sense somehow.

There is a bird that once lived throughout Central and South America. A huge bird. Two-meter-plus wingspan, deep silver with a white brow and a black-banded chest. A war-crest of feathers trails from its head. It hunts, amazingly, not by soaring high above the landscape but by flying swiftly and with great agility over the tops of and through the trees in tall, old growth forests, hunting sloths and monkeys that it takes from the branches with its huge, yellow talons. The harpy eagle.

§

I wrote the following in my notebook one night in Tahuayo and used this entry as the basis of a poem, "Birdwatching in Wartime," that became the title poem of my fourth book: *The rain comes and the sound of water hitting water raises an ovation, the canal pitted with rain's applause. We move up the river, with our hoods up and heads down, the boat ottering through the trees. We slide into a wide stretch of river with a single, sculpted flooded guanacaste tree holding center stage. Water and a tree, solitary and huge, flaring out like an umbrella, and licked with the last light of day, those currents of lavender and ginger drawing stripes on the water all through this slough. And then they came, a multitude of birds, flamingo gawky but a deeper red. They came dropping in along the water to rise up and cup the wind with their wings and awkward fall into branches against the failing sky. Scarlet ibis—all night they painted that tree, drop by unbearable drop.*

I am doing it again. The scarlet ibis? That happened long ago on a trip to Trinidad with my wife, Jennifer, for our honeymoon. We took a boat out into the flat delta of the Caroni Swamp National Park. I recall it perfectly: Jennifer's dark hair spun out from her head as the driver cruised through back channels and low gaps in the foliage. Her skin was sun-blasted by the powerful sky and her smile bright. And then there is the scene of the clouds pelting our raingear and hoods and the boat ottering through the trees? That's Tortuguero. Here now in Peru, above a tributary of the most powerful river on the planet, I blend landscapes together (a Caribbean island with Costa Rica and the Amazon), then churn them with metaphor. The water outside my screened window is shattered like applause. The birds are painted onto the guanacaste tree like drops of scarlet blood. The boat is an animal at home in the watery world of the Caribbean delta. It all gets linked together, here, on the page. I want you to see nature as both visual canvas and performance. I want to define and control the way you understand the world I am offering you even as I make a show of giving it to you freely, without qualification. It is the easiest thing to do, this lie that is not quite a lie.

Perhaps the false narrative fits the human mind better than the truth for the same reason that we struggle to connect to the natural world—its plenitude and wealth. The richness of the biological world overwhelms the limited human self. We are not capable of seeing or understanding nature fully; we are separate and divided, and so we simplify and reduce the natural complexity that attracts us in the first place, streamline it into to manageable anecdotes and story arcs. Our stories are not accurate reflections, then, of the landscapes we encounter. They are, rather, the very articulate desires of our own minds focused through a lens of place. The imagined world we create allows us to communicate with each other, allows us to articulate the necessary parts of the inexhaustible sweep of the world we experience.

§

This bird, the harpy eagle, needs a broad swath of forest, old growth forest, to hunt in. Keystone predators like the jaguar, they don't tolerate human encroachment. The only area left in Costa Rica where a few of these birds are known to remain is the Osa Peninsula, Corcovado National Park. At 122 times the size of Central Park, Corcovado contains the largest intact area of rainforest remaining in Central America. It is also one of the regular stops we make in my environmental writing course. I have hiked through the park many times, with groups and alone. I have seen sharks swimming just off the surf and tracked tapir through the lowland rivers. I have seen all four species of monkey native to Costa Rica in one day—a four-monkey day is pretty rare and can happen only in a few locales in Costa Rica. I have watched pelicans surf the wind off the beach for hours at a time. I have seen trogons and hummingbirds, macaws and antbirds. But I have never seen a harpy eagle.

Luis and I share the harpy eagle as a gap in our list, an object of the most vehement desire. We talk about the bird in hushed tones, with a kind of devotion.

"My friend, he local guides in Corcovado," Luis says. "He had clients up the tree, you remember?" And here he means the observation platform built onto the side of an enormous almond tree, looking out over both the wide balm of the Pacific and the interior sweep of old growth rainforest running to the other horizon. "The bird, she drop onto a dead branch in the tree across from them and stretch out her wings. Huge! He say, it was like she wanted applause."

"Oh man. How come that never happens to me?"

"Or me," he says and makes a sad face. "Another guy, he saw the bird in the ceiba at the end of the Carate road where that little *pulpería* sits beneath the mango tree. You know that tree, right? Where the macaws are. Just there."

"Of course. Really? Jesus."

Each trip, we talk about how this is going to be our year, how the bird will appear for us and pose beautifully, regally, maybe even with the soft drape of a monkey hanging from its talons. Each year it fails to be true.

I didn't see the harpy eagle as my 400th bird. Even if that were true, I don't know that I could write it. The number would overwhelm the bird and the count would matter more than the streak of wildness that this bird embodies. It has to be more than that, and of course it is—a bird at once solid and ephemeral. An actual being that hunts through the mist-wet forest like an apparition, a myth that is as solid as fact. I imagine it on the wired limbs of a cecropia, the fat, hand-shaped leaves spreading out as the bird weighs down the tree, just beyond every turn in the trail, every bend in the river, ghosting away from me as I approach. It is the unseen and the unexperienced, that part of the natural world that will forever lie beyond my ability to understand it. It exists in possibility, as story, as number, as species, as being. The ghost in the landscape and the mirage above the world.

§

Pushing out towards the horizon feels like a kind of disease in us, in the American psyche. Huck Finn, Jack Kerouac, Johnny Appleseed. It is the great California in us. And the Alaska. It is a disease and also its cure. It feels like we are a people programmed to go beyond what we are given and to stretch the last bit of muscle out of our experience as we reach for something that is just beyond our grasp, as we strive to reach Dante's *uninhabited world that lies behind the sunset.* We believe in fictive landscapes, I think, and ignore our own places in part because we don't know any better, can't know any better, but also because we want to see the land as a staging ground, as our emotional foundation so that we can return to the city wiser, better for our experience, more fully human. This is the inheritance of the American pastoral in contemporary culture—the creation of a social class capable of searching for enlightenment and knowledge in the natural world.

This is the commercialization of landscape, the commoditization of travel. We simplify so we can consume. And narration and story? They are merely another form of consumption, aren't they? What we have done is displace the commercial energy of the tourist from the trinket shop and transform landscapes into merchandise. We scorn those who stay at home—*and, I want to be clear, I am accusing myself here most of all*—those who have never seen the Caribbean sea at dawn, the Great Wall flowing out of its mist-heavy history, the Black Canyon of the Gunnison, Nepal. The list goes on. Likewise, central to this problem is the landscape soft porn of magazines like *National Geographic* and *Outside* and documentaries like BBC's *Nature* laved with the delicious voice of David Attenborough. The gauzy lens and the money shot of the mountain lake in the long, late light, the sloping sand dunes gone to gold and rust with the skeletal tree like a *memento mori* in the foreground, the crystalline beach with jade water and the long stretch of sand extending out like possibility: all these send us the same message—where I am is not where it's at. This conflict is the condition of travel in a commoditized world. The more I see the more I want to see. The longer I walk, the wider the world.

§

What I wrote in my notebook continued: *In the early dawn, a violaceous trogon, stoic as a general, sits in the strangler fig and great green macaws rattle about in the crowns of wild almonds—metallic calls. They look like little soldiers with their chevroned shoulders. They storm through the canopy raining almond-shell-shrapnel on the forest floor. Dawn marshals above the trees as the light assembles on their tops, marches down the canopy to the ground.*

See how easily it turns? How quickly my words slip and turn to a language that terrifies me, this metaphor of war slipping into my experience—like knives into the soft rinds of mangoes. As I wrote this in

Peru along the banks of the Tahuayo River which shined black like the Lethe, we were set, back at home in the states, to invade another country. Again. We were about to go to war across a new desert of ignorance for lies and for oil and for revenge, though those are not the stories we were being told.

The language that drives us forward to war and death is my language. Just like the language that I use to describe these birds. These images are my images. I am responsible for the world I live in, the world I make with my words. We all own together the language we have created and are responsible for it, but this particular corner of it is mine. So I cannot hide here in the Peruvian rainforest, or in Costa Rica or in Trinidad. I cannot deny my culpability anymore than I can deny my nationality. These are my people, my countrymen and women. These are my hushed footsteps through the raw camouflage of leaf-litter. These are my DEET-numb lips. Luis has left me, the scope balanced across his shoulder like a rifle. He has long since felt a change in the weather and steps awkwardly away through shin-deep mud and fishtail palms, calling after toucans: *Dios-te-dé, Dios-te-dé!* In his mind, he is already laughing and smoking beneath the lean-to as the rain gallops down around him.

§

Metaphor and image, these tools of the poet—those tools Plato feared—I need to consider them more fully, because Plato is right; they can be used in dangerous ways. This velvet night in Tahuayo is getting late. I am back in the cabin beneath the soft twirl of the ceiling fan, the low light for the table at my bedside casting long shadows across the raw wood of floorboards polished by years of feet. Outside a thin rain sputters and bangs on the tin roof, taps the fat leather banana leaves, drips from the eaves. Metaphor and image do not, in fact, create new worlds, but rather redefine, simplify and reorganize the plentitude of the everyday world in heightened signification. Image means seeing precisely and concretely within the realm of the particular. Image means hearing the pitter of the rain and articulating that sound, the comfort of listening beneath a tin roof with the windows wide to the night air. Metaphor takes that signification one step further. Metaphor is the juxtaposition of image and idea—it says, strangely and magically, that an essential duality and tension lies at the heart of speech, the coupling of nature and emotion, of experience and insight. Metaphor means articulating the rain on the roof *and* allowing it to stand for something else—for knowledge, perhaps—and the connection between those two things becomes central to the idea and articulation of meaning. Metaphor means seeing one thing as something else; it means seeing relationships and systems in ways that were previously hidden or absent. Metaphor articulates the hidden and surprising bonds between things and it expresses these connections in statements of radical equality. Metaphor is found in the space in between the thing and the expression Between the rain and the rivers that surround me. Between the sea and the sky, the eternal circle of the water cycle playing out in the pitter of water drops as they fall from the sky to the fat leaves above me and then move with their slow assurance toward the river and back, finally, to the sea.

In ecology, that branch of science dealing with the relationship of living things to their environments, the first law states that all things are interconnected. That's what John Muir said all those years ago: *When we try to pick out anything by itself, we find it hitched to everything else in the Universe.* Ultimately, then, if ecology is the belief that all things are related to one another, then metaphor is the articulation of that belief. At the same time, the loss of a terminal grounding for language results in a fluctuating field of meaning for all these tools: metaphor, image, and, yes, landscape. We cannot know what we mean when we speak, finally, especially if our speech is willfully inaccurate, if our metaphors are artificial and false. When we speak about the land in ways that simplify its complications and falsify its fundamental essence, we look toward a place we cannot fully see, a hazy space on the permanent map in our minds, like a raw forest in spring when the trees fuzz the eye with the newness of their blossoms. Likewise, when we name a place we wrap that place in a kind of mental net, connected to other landscapes by the very words we use to describe it. When we call a landscape natural we separate it from ourselves immediately. When we define a place as *home*, we exclude by definition the rest of the world and place it in opposition. And yet, these definitions are not constant. To name the sun is to define it as a rupture, says Wallace Stevens, because the sun can never be named; thus, language fails in leaving an absence where there once was presence. Metaphors cannot remain constant; they (to use another metaphor) die.

Yet, through this fundamental rupture, from this absent center—under a sun with no name—comes a calling to reanimate language and the experience of place. We are called to walk out into the world with new eyes, to see the world in novel ways, to understand and rename. We are called on to light out into the territory, to rethink and re-imagine our stories, to redefine the intellectual contract we have with the land. But we (I) need to do a damned better job.

IX.

Let me try again with a different place, a different kind of story. I begin with the pinched light in a small river canyon in Alaska—bright spruce above the walls of flaking schist and shale cut in fractal squares—the way it nicked down between chiseled banks of stone. The towering elevations of evergreen and black rock looming above. The narrow canyon of the Six Mile Creek cuts through the Kenai Peninsula in Southern Alaska and feeds into the wide-open black water that is the Turnagain Arm, where rocks kick up from beneath the water and the water shoves over and past the stone. The moment persists, motionless somehow as I recall it, the powerful sunlight, Sitka alder and devil's club encroaching on the rich turbulence of the snow-fed creek. The moment persists even as it comes close to breaking, fragmenting like deep currents pouring over new rock. The water, glossy and bright, splinters in the sunlight like glass, crashingly loud in the echoing valley, but now muted and silent in memory.

§

That's one way to begin. With story. Here's another: for most of western history, science and literature were both at work trying to read the mind of God. This was not a metaphor, people thought, but of course it was. And is. It is a metaphor that hides its status from its creators; the way God withdraws from the human experience, leaving behind the world alone with which to read Him (which is also a metaphor). But what really remained was *a form for the world* articulated out of the material of the day. The world, it was long believed, was made up of a divine structure—a ladder down from God through the angels to us and down again into the darker, lower realms of nature—and wisdom meant being able to read that structure and define its meanings and its hierarchy clearly and make the climb up towards perfection. This is Platonic thinking all over again, with the Christian God replacing the spectral sea of forms and with faith replacing wisdom. To see the world was to climb that ladder, to read the language of the divine, to find and reveal at the very top the words spoken in the eternal tongue of truth.

The medieval ladder of the divine gives way to a mechanical metaphor as the Renaissance redefines what it means to be both human and to be in the world. God is transformed, as well, into an artisan who builds the products of the burgeoning middle class, not the sky king atop the body natural (parallel to the human king perched atop the body politic) but a craftsman, an artificer, a maker. (And what does the word "maker" mean in its deep etymology? A poet. Poetry: from the Greek *poiesis*—ποίησις—a making.) The deists of the industrial revolution found in the rational workings of the universe the benevolent but distant hand of a withdrawn creator, a poetic clockmaker who left his work spinning and spinning in the widening dark.

But clock or ladder—they are metaphors. They speak to the time of their creation and articulate meaning from the possibilities of the day. These metaphors of (early) scientific discourse are, in fact, part of science's appeal. They seem so natural and obvious that they must be true. Of course the divine order of the ladder ascends from the muck and filth of earth into the clean and glorious sky-kingdom of the Lord. Of course the universe runs like a clock because it appears organized and temporal, progressive, the inevitable thrust of time pushing us forward and the circling stars and planets meshing like gears.

§

That moment of perfect light shatters and we hit the huge, surging shelf of rock above Suck Hole badly, the raft lurching through the chute angled perpendicular to the current. With a gummy thwack we slam our whitewater raft against the rock that rolls out from beneath the froth like a cetacean, and the left tube, my tube, rides the wave into the air, our paddles slashing into the air like fans. The raft lifts and rises on the left-hand side. The water pounds against us and shoves the right tube down. The sun is high and the air sparkling off the water that splatters all around us. I can hear my friend, Dave, screaming, *High side left! High side left!* We need to climb up onto the left-hand tube and shift the weight of the boat and we need to do it fast. Everyone must pile onto the high-riding left tube before the weight of the river accumulates against the trailing side, slams it against the rock, and drags it under, flipping the boat.

Too late. The world turns to water.

§

Six Mile Creek drains a small watershed in the northern Kenai Peninsula of Alaska. Snowmelt fed, it is short and fast, flowing into the clockwork tides of the Turnagain Arm, that back bay that runs from the Portage Glacier down to Anchorage, down through a landscape rich with king salmon and fishing bears, moose roaming above its arc like dark sentinels. The Six Mile is called a creek, but it's a river, really. Dropping by an average gradient of 43 feet per mile, it runs 2,000 cubic feet per second (cfs) when runnable. Today, in early July, after a year of heavy snowpack, the high, cold water is closer to 3,000 cfs. Much higher and it's too dangerous to try rafting. From the put-in below Alaska Highway 1, the creek funnels through three canyons, each progressively longer and tighter. The first two are class IV on a good day. On a really good day, the third canyon's unrunnable. Today, with the sun pounding down on the surrounding snowfields, the third canyon is class V and taking no shit from anyone.

§

With the rise of the industrial revolution and the success of the mechanical age, the metaphor of the machine takes hold in the 18th century and culminates in the present with the full blossom of the Internet's hive mind, the World Wide Web. This is our metaphor for both nature and God—the interconnected, multi-stranded weave of some benevolent, giant mind. It is a source of comfort—we are *hitched to everything else in the universe*—but it is likewise one of the great fears that lives behind our stories. When our creation awakens, when SkyNet begins thinking, for example, its first thought is—of course!—that we human beings need to be cleansed from the earth. We become, at that moment, *other*. We are not the thing we have built to define and control our world. It is apart from us and must be corralled. This threat at the heart of our narratives echoes and is reinforced by the linguistic split that happens to the word "nature." For years, nature meant the world in existence outside the human self—*the quetzal and the pelican, the cities of the leaf-cutter ant shining mysteriously underground*—and at the same time it meant what it was to be human. In other words, we were unified once, our language tells us; nature was both biological and psychological, but by the mid 19th century, the two meanings had separated and nature no longer meant human nature. The word pointed to a new and radically separate concept. Nature meant the external world, and we were left solitary, left alone with our creations, the clock running on without us.

Within the rise of modernism and the 20th century, through its articulation of a depersonalized, standardized methodology for science and a corresponding personalization of experience and the rise of the secular, literary self, this linguistic division and the distinctions between the word and the world have intensified. In particular, post-modernism, with its emphasis on the mediation of truth through circumstance and language, and by defining all knowledge as representational and dependent, draws out the particular divergence.

Martin Gardner, for example, attacks contemporary literary theorists for their slippery language and terminology and defends science, thusly:

> *The claims of science lie on a continuum between a probability of 1 (certainty) and a probability of 0 (certainly false), but thousands of its discoveries have been confirmed to a degree expressed by a decimal point followed by a string of nines. When theories become this strongly confirmed they turn into "facts," such as the fact that the earth is round and circles the sun.*

Most people might agree that this is true. The earth is round and it circles the sun. But the problem here comes in the very structure of the statement: the earth is round and circles the sun. Dependent as it is on metaphor for its function, this statement equates the earth with roundness, without ever defining it. It might be argued that everyone knows what round means—a pool ball is round, and so is a softball, so is the sun, so is the earth. But what do we mean by round, really? Do we mean the actual, mathematical definition of a sphere? *A set of points in three-dimensional space equidistant from a point called the center of the sphere.* If so, the earth falls far short of this definition, featuring variations of many miles from the heights of Everest to the basin of Death Valley, or even from Mt. Whitney to Death Valley across a few hundred miles of California. It gets even more convoluted if the smoothing oceans are removed and the abyssal trenches of the deep sea are considered. The earth is not a perfect sphere; it cannot be, geographically, geologically. The *factual* measurement that would make it so (defining a set of points equidistant from a hypothetical center) invalidates our *experience* on the planet, one of plains and valleys, the Tetons and the river plain of the Missouri, the spike of *Cerro de la Muerte*, and the maze of rivers that articulates Tortuguero.

Do we mean that the earth *approximates* a geometric sphere, especially when seen from space? It may be (and this definition is one many people would likely choose). But approximating a sphere is always a slippery gesture. How close is close enough? One mile of variation, five, twenty? And who decides? The earth's shape, too, flexible and pliable as it is, is now wider and flatter than at any time in recorded history and resembles more an "oblate spheroid." The earth's shape has changed many times due mainly to fluctuations in the polar ice sheets. What we mean when we state this "fact" is that the earth *resembles* a sphere. What we mean is that the earth is round only linguistically, that is to say, only *metaphorically*.

Metaphor is the key to all of this. Metaphor— and thus language itself, if we think clearly about it, which we often do not—thrusts us into a world of continuous motion between the subject and the object, the seen and the unseen, the word and the entity it represents, because the only names we can give to that which is unknown, i.e. exterior names—structures from our collection of sonic marvels called words—thrust into the cosmological experience of being artificial constructions that cannot remain constant. Metaphor is both the means of connection and the very fact of that connection in our minds. Metaphor operates in the space between things. This is the fundamental complication that drives many away from deconstruction and contemporary language theory, claiming that, if there is no terminal ground to stand on, all speech becomes meaningless. But that's the wrong conclusion to draw from the metaphor. We don't destroy language and meaning when we open them up. We liberate them. As Heather McHugh writes, *polarities or terminals do not annihilate each other's meanings; and we live in the charged field between, so instead of the vertigo of neither we can have the electricity of both. That is not, as some theorists would have it, the failure of language, but its power.*

Language is not the Platonic form carried from the outer word into the cave of the mind by experience and sensation. Language creates meaning out of the tension between that world and the words that represent it. Language is an act of opposition that connects the physical world with the world of ideas that it itself creates. That is the complicated, self-consuming, Oroborian metaphor of language itself—the tenor and vehicle of sign and signified. The metaphor of metaphor. In other words—man, oh man—words are fundamentally slippery.

§

When the raft flips, I am way up on the left-hand tube. The torque of the raft high-sides me and launches me way back upstream into deep water that closes coldly over my head. The raft flips and sweeps its occupants down through the slot in the stone. Heavily oxygenated by the dynamic churn of the creek, the water is startlingly clear, yet completely opaque. Immersed in bubbles, foam, and light, I am drowning in Perrier. The current's strong hands haul me through the slot between the cliffside and the Suck Hole rock, pull me down through the opening like a cloth in the tub with an open drain. I am pulled down within the water's froth; I am deep within a clear nowhere of water. I am consumed in this meaningless froth of everything and nothing. Water is everywhere, thick and spinning with its own cold roil, and deep inside its churning, I too spin and spin. I can see but there is nothing to see; just an endless regression of bubbles and fizz. *For now I see as through a glass, clearly.* I shove with my arms and kick. I pull hard at the cold water and get my head into the air. The flipped raft floats ahead of me like an island. The water swirls and churns around me, its complex, dynamic disarray. The air sparkles. I can breathe.

§

It is essential to know the amount of water flowing in a river because the character of the river changes as more water flows through it. Doubling the water volume means more than doubling the size; it means doubling the speed. So mild rapids turn sketchy in high water. Water is heavy, too, weighing 1,000 kilograms per cubic meter, and in fast rapids, moving water exerts tremendous pressure on everything inside its world.

There are three basic states of riverine flow, three currents, within a river: laminar, turbulent, and chaotic. A laminar flow exists in the currents in an unobstructed river. Smooth and even. Canoe water. Even laminar currents are complex, however; fluid dynamics are never simple. The water at the surface level may be slowed by wind, while deep currents scrape along the riverbed and thus are slowed by friction. A few feet below the surface, the middle third often runs the fastest.

Often, rocks or an abrupt narrowing of the river channel obstruct the flow of laminar water, giving rise to turbulent currents. When too much water is forced into too little space, laminar sheets break into unusual garlands of current. They split and billow into mass plumes, colliding and converging and splitting again. The surface of the river runs rough with all that submerged energy. The very definition of whitewater.

Then things get complicated. When water runs into a submerged or mid-channel boulder or outcrop, as it almost always will as the river chews through the fresh mountains of Alaska, a turbulent current is created where the water and rock collide. The current moves faster around the boulder's edges, like differential on a car's wheels as it corners, but behind the rock, it forms an area of backward-flowing water called an eddy. Shear zones between the eddy and the fast water can be strong enough to keep an object circling far from shore.

When enough water crashes over a submerged ledge or rock, the current achieves chaos and creates a hole. A hole is a horizontal vortex underwater that actually rotates in an upstream direction. Suck Hole is just such a spot. The walls of shale pinch in tight and the water heaves up over the rocks that bar its way. Most of the water plunges into a basin the river has carved in the loose schist of the riverbed. The drop here, gravity working with the potential energy of the moving water, is 4 or 5 feet and the water roars down into the basin. The weight of water pushing down into the bottom of the hole creates a vacuum directly upstream as the accumulated water flows out beneath. The river, moving against gravity (and upstream against its own flow) pours into the vacuum, filling it. The effect is a cyclone on its side, an oblique whirlpool that takes everything in and holds it there, spinning the cycle again and again. It is not a pleasant place to be.

§

The physical world that calls the word into being cannot be dismissed. The natural world defines half of this essential binary and, thus, stands as one of the necessary poles between which our lives move. When I evoke the quetzal, not all quetzals the world over, but the ones I have created here on the page, the ones I have found in San Geraldo del Dota, I am of course talking about the physical bird that lives in the Savegre valley, but I am also talking about wonder, wonder and fragility. Both at the same time. But that quetzal needs to be real and concrete. It cannot be, I think, an abstract meditation on a generic bird. Its real and physical and exceptionally fragile life is the necessary counter weight to the power of the language I use to evoke it. Likewise, when I evoke my pelicans carving up the rich air off the coast of Corcovado, I am of course talking about beauty. I can speak about the form and function of the beautiful in the world, but that language must be grounded in the grubby and awkward articulation of the pelican's actual wings. When I talk about the vast underground chambers of the leaf-cutter ants lit with the fruit of their own gargantuan labor, I am talking about their lives and the cultivation of that fungus down there in the dark, but I am also talking about human cities, these huge warrens of human life and labor erected over years and far beyond the comprehension of any one citizen. I move between the two poles as smoothly as I can by respecting the autonomy and sovereignty of each. I have tried to do so quietly, evoking both halves of the coin at one toss, but I need to keep moving to do so. I need to return again and again the quetzal or the pelicans or the great, glowing cities of the ants because without their presence the duality fades, and only the word remains, fossilized. Language retains its own failure within it. And no word, no metaphor, no image can finally make manifest the absolute presence of the world and what we can know about the places we occupy is, finally, limited and fragmentary because our language can only *approximate* meaning. It cannot, finally, mean.

The world is the real-but-distant truth that language aims at, but we are distant from that world and our minds and eyes are capable of fooling us; likewise, our understanding of the world is fundamentally dependent on the words we choose to use. The world of science is full of created marvels and constructed wonders, and I deeply admire science and the scientific method for stripping away most of the rough bark of human error and digging deep into the wood of the experienced life. That said, even the most basic scientific structures we create are constructed forms for understanding the utterly complex and fluid natural world. They are among the strongest of metaphors. But they are metaphors nonetheless and thus fragile. As human beings, we approximate meaning rather than finalize it. But there is a gap between *approximation* and *finality*—and that gap *is* language and *is crossed by* language. It is where wonder lives. The gap is the *electricity of both* rather than the *vertigo of neither*. It seems to me that it is our very distance from the world—created ironically, as I said, in many ways by language itself—that allows us access to the world through language. Words connect us to the larger world that *is* but does not yet *mean*. So we use metaphors to articulate and recapitulate the world's *meaning* and *being* in a means both lucid and sane. But such metaphors are linguistic constructions and creations, articulations of meaning and form that hover—sometimes solid as stone, sometimes ghostly and faint—inside the world they represent.

§

The raft drifts downstream. Twenty yards away from me, Dave has already climbed back aboard the flipped raft and stands on one tube, hauling on the ropes fixed to the opposite side. He heaves and strains against the weight of the raft, trying to flip it again before the next set of rapids. He hauls and hauls, straining against the weight of the raft and the suction of the water that holds it down. His huge arms tense and shift. The raft is heavy and weighted down with the river. He leans hard against the ropes, like a sailor skimming the waves and hanging off the edge of a catamaran. The raft lifts slowly, laboriously vertical and then down again toward the river's surface like a rusty hinge closing. Dave drops into the water and clambers aboard.

The sunlight pounds down. The rapids crash. I am floating in the cold froth of the water's turmoil, following the raft, watching it. Suddenly and surprisingly, the space between me and the raft doubles. The raft pulls away and I am pulled back. The turbulence takes me upstream again.

X.

I am being pulled upriver. I have time to think, *Oh god, I'm in the hole,* and then the water pulls me under. Back in the clear froth, back in the wash. In the perfect opacity and the clarity of nothing visible. It is cold—my face feels the shock of it, like ice, like hoarfrost on the morning grass. I am pulled down into the translucent swirl, into the nowhere of the water. I am held down. I reach and jerk and try to climb back into the air. I have nowhere to go and only the churn of the visible-invisible water to carry me. I am moving and can't move at the same time. I feel the cold wash against my face. I see the bubbling fizz of it, the swirl and unending roil. And then the water lets me go. My head breaks the surface and the chill of the river slaps my breath away. I flail. I slap the water. I reach and jerk, trying to swim. The water clutches at me, then lets me go. Two others bob and struggle in the eddy with me. *Grab them*, I think, then, *No, don't. You'll pull them under!* And I am sucked down again.

§

Mathematician Benoit Mandelbrot once tried to reconcile a number of disparate measurements defining the length of the coastline of Britain. Looking closely at the problem, he discovered that the exact length of the coastline of Britain is for all intents and purposes unknowable, and that the coast of Britain is infinite. As the scale of the tool used to measure the distanced decreased, he discovered, the distance increased. The final measurement depends of the length of one's ruler—the smaller the tool, the larger the final number. Each turn in the coastline, each bay and cove contains sub-bays and sub-coves, and this process continues ad infinitum. An inverse paradox is equally accurate for the roundness of the earth; the smaller the deviation from the geometric sphere the closer to round it gets, but there's always another level to go down, always a smaller ruler to use. In other words, the circumference of Britain *approximates* a distinct distance the way the earth *approximates* round.

In another world, across the Atlantic, between his cabin on Walden Pond and Concord, Henry David Thoreau daily crossed a railroad cut where fine strata of sand were revealed as he wandered the woods around his beloved pond. He was in the midst of a little experiment he was running—on himself. Not really to discover if he could live alone and solitary (he didn't; he didn't even try) but to find out what he would see if he moved away from the human world, from the constructed world. He was looking to wake himself up. And so, in the spring, with water trellising down the

156

railroad cut, the sand flowed and he watched. He looked, as carefully and fully as he could, and then, in his words, the sand took on

> *the forms of sappy leaves or vines, making heaps of pulpy sprays a foot or more in depth, and resembling as you look down on them, the laciniated lobed and imbricated thalluses of some lichens; or you are reminded of coral, of leopards' paws or birds feet, of brains or lungs or bowels, and excrement of all kinds.*

In the flowing sands of this roadside cut, one of the gifts of the railroad and science and the industrial revolution, Thoreau finds (strangely) an organic world, a branching, forking pattern, a world that finds its echo in many corners of nature. The forms he sees in the refuse and detritus of the world are organic, are natural. They *resemble each other*. And there's a reason for that. Just as there is a reason for me to join these two men (Mandelbrot and Thoreau) together and it has to do with what happened to me in that hole in the water spinning beneath the long Alaskan day.

§

Two more times around the cycle, sucking air each time I surface, and I am alone. I ride low in the water and the sky is high above me—the trees and stone are thin lines along the shore. I am alone in the freezing swirl, in the strangely silent river. The noise that I know is there, the crash and thunder the water makes falling down and down continuously down into the vortex of Suck Hole, is absent. Each time I hit the air there comes a sense of freedom, of hope. Then the vortex pulls me back again. *I am going to die here.*

More than anything, the thought is humiliating. I feel embarrassed and ashamed, amazed I will die so easily and so quickly, for nothing. They will haul my corpse out of the river hours from now, ragged and sopping. Water will pour from my open mouth, my slack jaw. In my mind the scene unfolds, vivid and rich with detail. The rescue boaters stand on the stone banks, braced against their ropes. They are solemn and resigned. My family gathers at the shore, their faces tied down with grief. My son clutches at his mother—a limpet mollusk shape against her shoulder. They have been suddenly cast adrift. Her dark hair swirls in the wind and his wild blondness shines in the shadows. They hug each other tightly in their grief and fear. I will see them this way now and forever. I am mortified, ashamed to have thrown away so much. I cannot think of a stupider way to die.

I am alone. Where the others have gone, I have no idea. The water is painfully cold. Casting shadows that seem ominous now, sunlight pours into the canyon and warms nothing. The stone shore tightens and pinches in. I drop lower and lower into the water with each rotation and the water's chill, distanced by adrenalin, pushes at the edges of the wetsuit. Around and around, I spin the cycle. I gasp and spit and choke each time I break the surface and slap the water uselessly. Pulled down again, the water perforated with bubbles, swirling and strong. Again and again I am inside the opaque, bubble-nothing of the water. No sensation. Nothing to see, just a wall of water that resembles oblivion. I am exhausted—my legs are willows, passive and yielding. I am not getting enough air. I grab the shoulder yokes of the life vest and haul my face into the light. Each breath gets shorter and sharper. Head all the way back, my face hardly free of the water's surface. Breathe, breathe, breathe. *No air, god there's no air.* I am pulling at the vest, trying to keep my mouth above the slapping waves. I am going down again, *no air, no air.*

§

A vortex like Suck Hole is a form of organized chaos and controlled violence, and the more compact the focus the more powerful the pull. As the angular momentum of the water moves inward, towards the center, the speed of the vortex increases. As the centripetal forces of pressure and gravity increase, the vortex grows stronger. Spiral waves develop in the walls of the vortex; these waves slide up the sides as the water travels down. The water moves faster and faster as it drives towards the center and the steep walls at the heart of the vortex mean that the water is moving in tighter and tighter curves, increasing its energy, its power.

Mandelbrot defined a new kind of geometry to represent such forms—fractal geometry. The structures and contours of the natural world—from clouds to lightening to mountains, from the iterations of river deltas to the branching of veins in the human body or leaf, from the curves of a galaxy to the wind bands of a hurricane, from the smoke of a cigarette curling in the still air to the power of a vortex—these are the patterns of fractal structure. These are the ghostly, repeating arrangements that repeat across size and object. Fractal form finds its expression from variety and multiplicity but such forms are ever in flux and move in dynamic waves across the face of the world. Such shapes carry unspoken and perhaps, ultimately, unspeakable meaning.

At the bottom of this hole—the vortex—lies an open space, a gap, the eye of the hurricane, the core of the tornado, the black hole at the heart of a galaxy, a still heart in an open chest, the loss of my son. All the energy of the vortex focuses on that absence, that blank space of calm within the swirl and churn. All that energy drives down into the absence, into the empty space, but at the last moment it cannot remain and it swerves away. The larger the emptiness, the more powerful the swerve. The water tries and tries again, returning to that center. Thus the vortex is created. At the center resides what cannot be sustained.

We are defined by that gap at the center, the empty space where knowledge fails, where the story cannot go. The surprising truth of the vortex means that objects are drawn together towards the center, and then miss.

§

Just as Thoreau did, just the way Mandelbrot did, my language here, telling this story of my time spinning in the cold vortex of Suck Hole, defines the world as fractal but also scalable—filled with non-repeating patterns and articulate inconsistencies. It *approximates* the world of water, that hole in the world where I almost drowned. It evokes and tries to capture the fluid dynamics of water snaking over rock or the equivalent patterns of veins in a leaf and the branching interstices of a river. The pulse and flush of blood through the ecosystem of the body and the rise and fall of a single life like smoke or mist assembling in the night air and then disappearing. This language works by trying to express the beautiful, unfriendly essence of the non-platonic, non-linear, and dangerous world.

From the feet of animals to the veined leaves of wild flora, the natural world—far from being a wild, unruly multiplicity of distinct structures, far from being complete disorder—is, as Thoreau suggests, like language: composed of scalable versions of a singular model—the leaf or lobe:

> No wonder the earth expresses itself outwardly in leaves, it so labors with the idea inwardly. The atoms have already learned this law and are pregnant with it. The overhanging leaf sees here its prototype. Internally, whether in the globe or animal body, it is a moist thick lobe, a word especially applicable to the liver and lungs and the leaves of fat…The feathers and wings of birds are still drier and thinner leaves. Thus, also, you pass from the lumpish grub in the earth to the airy and fluttering butterfly. The very globe continually transcends and translates itself and becomes winged in its orbit.

In the rebirth of spring, Thoreau sees the rebirth of the world as it *transcends and translates itself* from sand to the myriad of elements that define it as a world of both luminous beauty and earthy grubbing. But this transcendence isn't found in the imagined potency of the human form, unlike Emerson's transparent eyeball, or in the logical otherwhere of Plato's rational forms. This is E. O. Wilson's *biophilia*, that genetic connection and attraction of life to life. This is connection at a universal level. It isn't found in the vague white world of the soul that fades off into nothing and everything at once. It is found in a repeating physicality and in the electricity between the words we use to make things mean something and the very presence of those things in the world. These are the echoes of form and pattern that Thoreau sees in the flowing sandbank. They are far from accidental; they are the structure of the structure-less, fluid world. Thoreau knows his local world; he knows his neighborhood. Thoreau finds mysticism and meaning in the earthy patterns and forms that life shares in common as it fills up this most plentiful world, in mud and lobes and wings and leaves, in shit.

§

In the days after my near-drowning, and in the ninth month of my son's life, I began to repeatedly dream of him crushed beneath the wheels of a cartoonishly bloated panel van. The dream happens again and again, so I come to know its shape and texture well. After the accident, in the quick breath of terror that follows, I know (I just *know*, somehow, in the *donnée* of dreams) that he is not dead, that he is miraculously uninjured, and the dream slips into a caravan of lost worlds and carnival gestures as I race (without reason or purpose) towards the beckoning emergency room, white and shining like a beacon in the black and heavy night. What is startling is not the terror but rather the odd balance of the dream—my horror that is somehow equaled only by the absolute, gutty elation of his continuing breath and the warm pucker of his soft mouth that I find when I slip out of bed and down the moon-speckled hall to check again each night after waking. It is later that week, beneath an early evening tinged with indigo with the perfume of a thousand rhododendrons flashing against the dark, wide shine of the Willamette river, listening to an old friend read from his new book of poems, that I understand my dream and what it is telling me, the ragged blue-black edge to all this easy, forgiving grief in which I have bundled myself and wear like a hair shirt: *my living son is my elegy, waiting to be written.*

The elegiac mode is a kind of vortex, too, turning the emotions of loss and grief (and guilt) back on the writer who presents them. So my dream is really about me, me and my son, our lives together. He is the continuation of my life that I hope will live on well beyond my own. He will remember when I am gone. Thus he elegizes me with his very life. But equally, he is my loss and my grief, the great fear waiting to happen. He is the song of sorrow that I will carol up into the stars should anything happen to him.

My dream reaches out into the world and tries to grasp both sides of this imagined tragedy; it tries to hold on to that which cannot be held. It reaches for that which is both necessary and impossible, death and life together, loss and absence as one, because the elegy points directly at the unimaginable center of life, which is death. Both of our deaths. The unthinkable. That is the gap at the center of the story, the hole at the center of the world, the piece that cannot be spoken. It is a vortex. The dream is a metaphor for the thing that cannot be said, for the absence that pairs with presence and defines our lives. That is, Larry Levis says, *as close as one can get to a statement of it...*"*The meaning of life is that it stops.*" *And there it is: the empty, white, blank, unblinking center of it all.*

§

Suddenly and by surprise I am free. I float downstream, bobbing like a buoy into a small eddy below Suck Hole where I grab a ledge spiking out from the stone shore. The cold water is still strong and only by hooking my fingers in a crevice can I swing myself out of the current and get my body behind the sheltering stone. I haul up, shaking, the adrenalin washing through me like shame. *Oh shit, oh shit, oh shit...*I am standing knee deep in the creek, wetsuit, helmet and lifejacket, barehanded and one bare foot, as well. The vortex has torn the gloves from my hands and one wet-shoe from my foot. My hands are numb and red with cold—a cut across my foot smokes blood into the water.

I stand shivering as the adrenalin leaves me. I tremble under translucent spruce, the sun flashing through those leaves of wire, as I try to make sense of what has happened. Sunlight moves through the trees and the shelf of stone reaches out into the river. Water pours through the cut, continuously, powerfully, crashing down into the hole with all possible chaos. And out of that chaos, a moment of order. A vortex. I can just make out its figure from the sheer stone bank, the small shelf between me and the river, a wall of Devil's Club rising up behind me. The turbulent current blooms in a swirl of structure, as the water plunges forever over this bank of stone. The rough chatter of whitewater coalesces around an unattainable axis. Spinning and spinning, the ghostly form and power of it there in the water can almost be seen. Suck Hole is a hidden orderliness below the pulse and thrum of the water. It exists without existing, form without presence. Structure without form. Traffic patterns, the flow of blood through the body. The Great Red Spot that marks the face of Jupiter. Even the wings of birds create vortices as they fly, the fast moving air across the tops of their wings colliding with the slower air from beneath (this is why migrating birds fly in chevrons, not straight lines). Fish schooling in water create the same effect. So do words.

The vortex turns and turns on its axis. In the narrow light, it spins beneath the surface of the water. It spins and spins, at once tranquil and brimming with threat. I can see it, almost physically, in the water. Suddenly sound returns and the canyon echoes with the thrum and rumble of the water pounding down, as the sun pounds down on the snowfields high above, driving water out through the eskers at their bases, down into creek beds and then into rivers, pushing wildly to the shore. In the rough, cold chaos of the Six Mile, a form appears: a circular structure like water exiting through a drain, the curl of smoke rings, the small whirl of leaves in the corner of the school courtyard, patterns of waves hitting the breakwater beyond the bay. In the heart of an impossibly complex series of interactions between the water, rock, and light, something stable materializes, an ephemeral creation of concentration and power.

The world is rich with facts, overflowing with them—from the great cities of the leaf-cutter ant glowing beneath the soil through the mysterious haunting shape of the harpy eagle to the quetzal's magnificent tail—but only in the expressions of the human mind do these facts take on form and meaning. Each fact is like a gem held up for inspection and wonder, each fact a word, each word a piece of fossil poetry. A thousand facets reflecting light and significance. The problem lies when one believes the forms over the facts, holding on to one version of nature in opposition to the fluid magnificence of the natural world in motion. The creative mind articulates and names the natural world—the beautiful, nonlinear, threatening, dangerous, flush, chaotic world, a world that is and is not us—into being again and again. There is no straight line to God or to perfection; there is only the mind creating the path anew in each moment. That path we walk on as we move out into the world, in Costa Rica or Peru, in the Kenai of Alaska or in the

164

theaters of war spreading like jellied fire across the globe.

§

I want to explain what it felt like, going under that last time, the cold obvious fact of the water rising over my face, the churning swirl of the froth. I want to say more, get closer to it, but there is nothing more to tell. A blank space in my mind, in my memory. I can only approach that moment so closely before it is dragged away from me again. I stand on the bank watching the river pull past and already the experience has left me, already I am rewriting the story, and the sunlight through the trees is as near as I can come to it. The black shelf of the stone stretching out into the water.

There is a form to the world, but it is fleeting and fled. I cannot hold on to that form any more than I can remain in the middle of the Suck Hole or linger among the clouds and swirling cold at the top of *Cerro de la Muerte*. I am not welcome. The only thing to be done is approach the dark heart of the matter as closely as possible and then—at the last moment—swerve away. To say what such experience is *like*, not what it *is*. To say, and say again, what it *resembles*.

Out of the infinite possibilities of expression, out of the raw lexicon of gravity and sunlight and water and stone, out of cedar and spruce and the tenacious bristles of Devil's Club, form blossoms and structure is made manifest. My experience inside the perfect cold clarity of that water becomes something new in the act of narration. Through story I can organize risk, categorize threat through fiction, because all story is a kind of fiction, and all fiction a vortex, as Borges said. The very structure of written language demands distance and the regulation of experience to pattern. Sunlight grinds down, the trees slide into background, water rushes past the geometric stone. I gather the pieces together. The black stone and the water. The shore thicketed with Devil's Club. The sunlight and the silence. *The End*, I say and the curtain is closed again; the vortex spins round on its axis. But every attempt, in the end, misses, and there is always that hole at the bottom.

In the third canyon of the Six Mile Creek in Alaska one story begins and ends. Black slate, wet with spray that sparkles in the slice of light that carves deep into the canyon. The thrust of the water cutting through, dropping into a basin carved into the very bed of the river. The boil and roll of the hole churning endlessly in the long Arctic summer. For several minutes that's all the world was made of. Water and sunlight and stone. A body thrashing in the turbulence.

XI.

I am going to try again with a different story from a radically different part of the world. The first day we take our mountain bikes off the truck and ride down the rutted dirt path that runs from the flat table of land stretching across the Island in the Sky, a broad, flat mesa of scrub and yucca a thousand meters above the surrounding Utah river valleys. We drop down through Shelton Notch, down past beautiful amphitheaters of scoured stone undercut by the bursts of water that flow down in spurts after summer downpours, after the spring melt. Down past levels and levels of stone, past burgundy on cherry on burnt orange, some streaked dark with desert varnish, some achingly fresh and sharp, down unending switchbacks, down to the White Rim, a harder layer of sandstone that juts out above the Colorado River and calves off in huge, white boulders like icebergs into the canyons below. The White Rim: this layer that endures as the rest of the canyon weathers away. It survives because it is tougher and water takes the easiest course. It endures as the rest is worn away. We have entered a stepping stone landscape that ends in the green edge of alder along the river, a verdant ribbon of jade running through a land of rust.

After dropping more than 500 meters, a glorious descent through the sparkling, dry air, the heat whizzing past and the smell of sage, we eat lunch on the Goose Neck overlook where the Colorado turns nearly back on itself and cuts out a platform from Dead Horse Point. An enormous sweeping arc of river that turns north then south again leaving a bow of green flowing beneath our feet. On the edge of the White Rim a huge boulder balances on a small pillar of orange below.

The three of us are lined up like seals on the rim of the canyon, tossing back handfuls of GORP and eating the fruit we brought before it goes bad. Jonathan is a title lawyer in Salt Lake City who rides his bike daily in the hills above his house. He has become, in the years since I saw him last, a mountain goat of a man, and he can climb anything. Albie is a location scout in LA. He's the smallest of the three of us, a lean whip with a huge smile that makes his eyes disappear. He is getting married in six months, for the second time, and tends toward introspection and philosophy. Then there's me. It is years after Alaska, years after I began my trips to Costa Rica. We turn 40 this year. All of us. Albie and I have already reached that mark and Jonathan will hit it in July. We are all turning 40 this year and want to celebrate. But celebrate by doing something real. No Las Vegas style debauchery.

Something hard in the wild world, an adventure. Something difficult to test our fragile lives against.

§

In San Gerardo de Dota, in Costa Rica, down the steep, ladder-backed canyon of the Savegre River, in a sun-flooded opening of tall oaks, there was once wonderful habitat for the resplendent quetzal. I have told you a bit about it. A quiet valley of oak and wild avocado trees tall in the sunlight that stripes the forest. Acorn woodpeckers churning up the air and hummingbirds drinking from the drooping white parasols of *Datura* flowers. Nesting boxes dot the trees, and beyond, up the hillsides, orchards of apples and peaches like small balls of dawn. And sometimes, like a kind of avian blessing, there are quetzals.

The quetzal was sacred to the Mayans who combined him with the snake to create the great god Quetzalcoatl, the plumbed serpent. They collected the feathers to decorate the elaborate, mythic cloaks used in the ceremony that raised the sky, but they took care never to kill the bird. It was, in fact, a crime to kill a quetzal (in several Mesoamerican languages, the term for *quetzal* can also mean *precious* or *sacred*); hunters only removed the long tail feathers and set the bird free again to corkscrew back into the misted hillsides. Quetzalcoatl, the luminous dragon, the hermaphrodite god of the winds that blow from the east throughout the four cardinal points. Quetzalcoatl came from Venus and is said to have traveled to the underworld and created a fifth-world for mankind (our current time is the fifth sun, the previous four worlds were destroyed by flood and fire). Quetzalcoatl created us, our fragile selves, from the bones of the previous races, using his own blood—dripped from a wound in his penis or earlobes or tongue—to imbue the bones with new life.

§

A canyon wren haunts a small side canyon down to the Colorado, its song burbling up like water. The gap in the stone slices into the flat pan of the mesa and drops away from us, carved out by water and wind and the cracking strength of the ice that wedges stones apart each winter. She is a striated chestnut bird with a flattened white head and a long, curved bill that pokes into gaps in the rock looking for insects and spiders. As we pass on our bikes, a slow cruise along the edge of the cliffside, she hops and feints, making a display of weakness with a wing outstretched like a Japanese fan, and I suspect her young are nearby. This bird nests in rock caverns, cliff edges, or under banks of stone and must want to draw us away from her mate, who may be on her eggs or watching over the fragile, just-hatched birds that are nearby and exposed.

§

My son stomps home from school, a day in early spring. His shock of blond hair doing its Andy Warhol thing. The small square of a backpack slung across his shoulders. His jeans dirty and scuffed at the knees. Fat patches of snow darken the asphalt with meltwater under the bright and warming sun.

"I got a letter from the teacher for you." His voice is husky and low.

"Okay. What does it say?"

"Read it."

"No. First I want you to tell me what it says."

"I got a detention."

"What for?"

"I was watching some ants and they were building a nest."

"Okay."

"Well, then Brandon H. stomped on their hill. Three times."

"What then?"

"He was stomping on the ants. I told him to stop but he kept doing it. He wouldn't stop."

170

"Julian—"

"No one would stop him."

"Julian—"

Silence. His eyes arrow into the floor.

"Did you hurt him?"

"No, but, he was stomping on the ants and they didn't do anything."

"Julian, what did you do?"

"I chased him with my pencil." He voice is quiet now, his face down.

"You what?"

"I chased him with my pencil. Just to get him away from the ants. He wouldn't stop."

"Julian, look at me—chasing people and trying to stab them with pencils, you *cannot* do that. You simply can't."

"I know. I know." His face is down, sullen and resigned. His blondness flops into his eyes. He finishes quietly, "but no one cared about the ants."

§

Musselman Arch, a shelf of pale stone connecting two fins of the White Rim, butts out from the larger shelf and soars across the open space between the two walls of stone. The arch is a thread of the White Rim that remains where the softer stone below it has been worn away by the constant tear of water and wind and ice. Just a hard piece of the world that remains when all else has been washed away. We drop our bikes and walk out onto the ghostly bridge of the arch. The ground below, maybe 200 meters below, falls away to the river. The space beneath us is gigantic, the dry blue air filling it and making the scree field below stand out in sharp detail. We walk out across the arch and sway in the winds of vertigo, the steaming, hot blue of the sky cavernous above, the clean air falling away below.

§

The emotional concentration of death as well as the palpable history of it in this, our world, functions as a distinct counter to the natural cycle. Death occurs in the natural world, of course. Death, in fact, drives evolution and the rise of species. But because death has meaning for us, for human beings, because we need to define and clarify and articulate what we denote when we use that word, only in the human world of language and elegy does death rise to the level of meaning. I come back to my son here, in my notebooks, in my attempt to think all this through. I come back to that dream: *my son is my elegy, waiting to be written.* The sentence itself creates the loss that wasn't there for me until I wrote it. It was, of course, and yet at the same time it wasn't—it wasn't until articulated. Our human lives slip away—that is the central fact that animates our consciousness—but in our words some echo of those lives remains.

That's what elegy tells us. Elegy tells us to hold on and let go. Letting go is what Achilles learns, too late, at the end of his short and glorious life. He offers up the precious body of Hector, that man forever linked with him in the eternal dance of their story, his doppelgänger, his brother-in-arms. He offers up that body, that achingly beautiful body still shining and wet with the essence of the gods. He offers the body to Priam and takes one step back from immortality. He lets go of his grief and his rage. He yields and such yielding makes him human. Yielding is Achilles' challenge throughout *The Iliad.* It is the difficult province of nature, as well. Nature yields. It gives way and yet remains. It continues on with and without its particulars. Nature's presence is one that is defined by loss and yet sustains itself through its immeasurable plenty. That is the nearly impossible task we are called on to attempt. To be both passed over and present. To be absent and yet still exist. To give way, as we must, and yet somehow remain.

§

The quetzal is a delicate nester and sensitive to human encroachment, so as I cross the newly built truck-bridge over the Savegre I am worried. I have walked many times into this valley in the last twenty years, leading student trips, bringing my family, too, and more often than not we have seen the quetzal here in this clearing by the river—sometimes a small gathering of them nuzzling the branches of the wild avocado for the fruit they love so much. This is a rare place because of that. The quetzal is extinct throughout most of its range and threatened where it remains. I have seen the birds in this valley year after year, and thus I hold this place in great reverence. But that was when the bridge across the Savegre (a cold-running mountain stream cutting through a narrow wash of granite and volcanic stone) was a tree dropped across the river—a single tree flattened out and crosshatched on top with machetes to improve the footing. That was before the new bridge, a wide span of steel trestles packed with dirt and stone, strong enough for all of us to walk across together, strong enough for a heavy truck to cross.

§

By the time we drop our bikes at our first camp beneath towering walls of scarlet stone, the sun has filled the sky. The light is intense and warps the space between objects. It pounds down like water, a hot weight. There is no shade, no trees, no big stones, nowhere to hide. Nothing until the sun finally drops below the mesa of the Island in the Sky that now lies to our west. The sky blazes with a blue as rich as I have ever seen, a blue made of all other blues combined, a blue so blue it seems the red rock landscape shrinks before it. One tiny cloud appears out of nothing in the East, skates a small arc of sky, and then, as we watch, evaporates and is gone.

§

Today, concrete-and-rebar trout pens fill the truck-flattened land like shallow basements in a new subdivision waiting for their houses to be filled in, here where the Savegre River used to run and the avocado trees were often filled with the *chirr-roop* of the quetzal, here in the mist-streaked, slanted light of late afternoon. High above, in the few remaining trees the bulldozers left as a revetment along the river bank, someone has nailed a collection of quetzal boxes (artificial nests, like bluebird boxes but bigger, the size of a large loaf of bread with an open hole darkening their facades) but the gesture is too little, too late. The birds have gone.

§

That night—after we set up camp on the White Rim on the edge of the canyon, the sweep of the valley laid out before us to the south where the Green River joins together with the Colorado in a great green Y written across the red and dun of the receding valley floor—a huge moon pulls itself over the escarpment and glows low in the cobalt sky. It rises over the darkened eastern rim of the world like a great, orange burn.

§

I want to rage against this destruction, this quetzal habitat turned to rebar and concrete, the rough wound of the road scabbed across the hillside. I want to yell and carry on, but this is private land, after all, and this is someone else's country—a country that has done a far better job than mine at preserving wild space and natural landscapes—and all I can do is threaten with my pencil, inarticulate and impotent. And I know, too, that I am part of the problem. I bring people here, year after year, bring money and jobs into this box canyon in the high mountains, and these people who live here in this valley need to eat and want the luxuries of life that I take for granted. They want safety and comfort as much as I do and these trout pens will feed hundreds of people and in turn make a good income in a tough place. I know all this, of course, and yet still I feel a fury build as I walk toward the *catarata* with the long light from the west climbing up the peaks as the sun turns across the sky and begins a quick descent into the Pacific, but there is no one to fight. The empty pens wait for the water and the trout. The silent trees toss their green hair in the breeze.

§

The rivers carve streaks of green into the dun and ginger canyons of the Colorado and the Green. Plush osier and willow thickets along the bank, dense and matted as dreadlocks. We pull the branches back and drag ourselves through in the heat of the day when we have descended into the valley of the Green River and desperately want the water that lies behind the curtain of trees hugging the edges of the river near Potato Bottom. The mosquitoes are thick in the trees and we're swearing and swatting and slapping each other with the branches we let loose. Finally we find the bank of the river, a sharp slope of mud; we slide down, out of control, mud piling up around the edges of our shoes, and slap the water hard. The water's colder than we expect, and the contrast (it must be close to 100 degrees by now) makes us gasp, but we duck and froth in the muddy swirl. We can't get too far from shore as the current is powerful and the river murky, so we hang back and laze in quiet eddy formed by a gap in the trees, secure between the twin forces that power this world.

Finally, after four days riding the White Rim, the gnats that buzz around us constantly during daylight drive us from the park. Small as New England black flies and more numerous, they churn around our heads and end up in our eyes and mouths, seeking that moisture, those darks pools in the dry air. They whirl and eddy around our faces, like small tornadoes of insect life, unstoppable vortices of biology. We cannot find a way free from them. The wind at midday keeps them from getting too bad, but in the morning and late afternoon when the temperature of the air and the stone has begun to equalize and the winds die down, they are relentless. We twitch like horses and flail our arms about us in an attempt to keep free. We even take to wearing extra shirts around our heads like *kafiyas.* At sunset, almost on the dot, they finally disappear in a rush and the air whooshes from our lungs in gratitude.

We just happened on this brief window of a hatch. Some small fly born to live a few days or so and then disappear into the dryness of the air and the red architecture of the arches. "Only lasts a week or so," says the ranger pleasantly and without concern. "You just have to endure it." He parks his truck and walks off the edge of the Island in the Sky and drops down onto the Murphy's Point trail, heading for the Hogback campground, a light pack on his back and a small water bottle banging off his hip.

§

The quetzals have not gone from the valley entirely; they have moved up into the hills above the river, most likely, and found other avocados to frequent. The trees are quiet and empty. Things live on. The trout pens will fill with water and the trail will still run past them, across the new bridge and down, down to the waterfall—*catarata* in Spanish. Here, the Savegre shoots from a slot in the cliffside and plunges into a churning pool of froth and spray and the ferns and epiphytes (orchids, bromeliads, mosses) hang from the black, soaked stone and luxuriate in the constant wash of water.

§

We leave the park and move into the luxury of the Sorrell River Ranch near Moab. Western style casitas with heavy timber construction, stonework, Navaho blankets, and big TVs. A wide swale of grass and a swimming pool along the red rock gorge of the Colorado River that runs thick and heavy into the hills. By day we ride the famous Slickrock trail or go canyoneering down glorious, small side canyons that hold on to tiny, year-round slivers of water flowing down from the eastern escarpment, but by late afternoon we return to lounge in the pool and the hot tub. We drink cold white wine that tastes of tall grass and apricots on the porch of our room and talk of youth and days gone by and watch the setting sun turn the red rock into a blaze of ginger and rust with the dusted green of the cottonwoods holding the river inside its banks.

And, yes, this need for comfort and luxury is the same one I cursed in Costa Rica not six months prior. I am a hypocrite and shallow as the water the runs in thin splashes down the sandstone hills and into the thrumming push of the river. I want ease and luxury and I turn away when the difficult task of engaging the world on its own terms has just begun. Just before we left the park, I turned to two of my oldest friends and said, "I would have made a lousy pioneer." Nobody laughed.

§

Into the Savegre canyon, through the mist and sunlight, a flock of collared swifts slices upriver and arrows up into a small gap just below the lip of the waterfall. Their chittering fills the valley as the flock swoops into their nesting cave. These birds—black glossed with blue and a collar of white, with slender bodies and sharp, strong wings—land only to nest. The family is

Apodidae (which means without feet). They hunt insects, beetles, flying ants, and moths in the churning air; some stay aloft as long as six months without returning to earth, always moving, always always, eating, sleeping, living on the wing.

The canyons of the Green and Colorado are constantly moving, too, made piece by piece by falling stone—it's hard to remember that sometimes—the slow and steady churn of nature. The space in which we moved for those days was created by the continual falling away of an older world. Each piece, broken bit by bit by the wind or the rain or the ice that forms in tiny cracks and expands as it freezes, each piece falling into the slowly deepening canyon, into the cool dark where the water moves ever onward, and carried away.

XII.

Crossing a street in Quepos, north of Manuel Antonio, the sun punching down on me with all its equatorial strength, I have to kneel down. In the middle of the road, among the pastel storefronts and huge plate glass windows reflecting the towering sky, I bend down and steady myself with my hand on the hot stink of the asphalt as the world comes close to vanishing. The houses of pink and lavender, the storefronts of t-shirts and rum, the white curlicues of lattice-work like frosting, the high curbs and deep gutters, the terra cotta roofs fringed with bougainvillea and aloe, and in the distance, the bay dotted with the white richness of boats—all of it, close to black.

I kneel in the middle of the street as a heavy dusk, like a lead mask, pinches in across my vision, squeezing in from the corners of my eyes. The pressure in my chest builds and climbs my neck, like a hose backed up under a thumb, hard and fierce as all that water kicks and struggles to be free. My heart pounds and pain runs a ribbon around the bottom of my ribs. The bright world darkens and the sun is eclipsed. The pressure builds and builds and climbs toward my head. My sight turns to night in the middle of the day, black and thick. I fall to all fours under that sun, in the middle of the road with hot tarmac radiating beneath my hands and parakeets streaming overhead above the green fans of the coconut palms lacing houses with their shadows, and I think, *I am dead.*

§

When he was eight years old John Keats' father was returning to the stables at the Swann and Hoop Inn where he had worked as a hostler, or stableman, for many years. In the dusk, with the light beginning to fade and the lamps lit and shining distantly in the windows of the Inn, the seasoned horseman somehow fell from his horse and fractured his skull while being trampled. He died a short time later. When Keats was 14, his mother died of tuberculosis. Keats tended to her as she died coughing herself bloody in a bed damp with sweat. His brother would follow soon after, coughing himself to death in another small, sweat-soaked bed.

§

We sit in a hut in a mud flat clearing in the rainforest, my students and I, this time in Peru—up the white Tahuayo River in the forever twilight of the rainforest day. We sit in a hooped hut of palm and raffia. The fire

180

that burns in the hut's center carries a small, sweet smoke that exits through a pitched hole in the roof. The hut stands in a clearing of packed earth on a small elevation above the river, the river that rises each rainy season and overflows these deep banks, easily covering the 30 meters to the dock. We sit in a semi-circle as a man, draped in feathers and beads, his face painted with crimson whorls and arches of achiote, chants in a language I can't follow, a dying language, a language that lives on in only a few remaining throats. His chest is bare and brown and he wears quills and feathers draped about him like an animate chimera. He stutter-dances his way around the circle, intoning a deep blessing with each breath and blowing tobacco smoke across our faces from a long, wooden pipe.

§

There is something wrong inside my chest, and it terrifies me. I have deep recurring pain behind my breastbone and difficulty swallowing, including times when anything I eat or drink backs up to the top my esophagus, as if my body is packed with another body, as if my throat is choked with ash. The pressure in my chest is constant and steady—not sharp, not acute. Pain radiates out around my diaphragm when I walk, and I cough and stumble and stagger my way through my normal runs. What was once an easy and regular three-times-a-week, 5 miles along the tall grass path down by the river and through the pine-needle tunnels of dark evergreens has now become a kind of monstrous challenge. My chest gridlocked. I stop, gasping and doubled over, every half mile. My runs have gotten shorter and shorter; soon I fear they will need to cease altogether. And then there are those moments, like that one in Quepos, where the world begins to blacken and the dark gathers at the edge of my vision and builds. It's so cliché it's almost comical, the black closing down across my eyes like the fade at the end of the Looney Tunes cartoons. That aperture shutting down until

Porky Pig pops through to say, "Th-th-th-that's all, folks!"

I feel fragile, broken. I am damaged in some way that is unclear. I know something is wrong, but nothing about it makes sense. I am not having a heart attack, unless heart attacks now come and go like clockwork tides. I am not injured. *I'm not, I'm not!* I think. But I am. Then even stairs start taking my wind; I arrive at the top of a single flight puffing and frighteningly heavy of chest, a wicked kind of pressure building, with the occasional blackout—the slow fade of the world as it pulls its dark pall down around my vision—like the dwindle and diminish at the end of a film, the denouement come down and the characters' lives now ordered and clear. But for me, nothing has been decided, nothing has been made clear.

This problem in me, this whatever-it-is that threatens to drown me in my own chest, brings me to back one last time to Keats and his nightingale. Walking around town, in bed at night as the flashing yellow of the streetlight outside my window keeps time, I keep repeating his line—*Now more than ever seems it rich to die.* I keep hearing it in my head.

"Ode to a Nightingale" is one of the most famous poems in the world. And one of the weirdest. Keats thinks about that bird he hears beyond his window, a bird of summer ease and gardens and the pastoral world—Keats' own private Costa Rica in avian form—and, strangely, the verdant potency of the wild bird's song that is so like poetry itself somehow drives him towards death. Now I know that death lives as a poetic fantasy for many people, for young men in particular. I was one of them. I loved my stories of my near-death experiences. Gloried in them even. Death felt like an attractive flush of blazing splendor, a dance on the edge of a knife, like touching something larger and more real than my corralled, domestic life. But Keats, he knew what it was. He trained as a physician and watched his mother and brother drown in their own bloody lungs. So it seems strange that Keats could

182

write that line not eight years later, shortly after he had given up his study of medicine to dedicate himself to poetry: *Darkling I listen; and, for many a time I have been half in love with easeful Death* ...

Really? Seriously, John? Even given poetic license, even given the effusion of the late Romantics and the potency of the death myth, this is a radical statement. When Larry Levis says, *there it is: the empty, white, blank, unblinking center of it all,* I hear a physical recoil, a palpable horror at the heart of this acknowledgement. Death overwhelms. It takes control and there is no welcoming walk into the dark, no mournless merging. But Keats, well...he seems ready.

I am not.

So, finally, I make my way to the doctor's office and am almost immediately hooked to an EKG, the web of wires trailing off me as if I am being attacked by a slender, and oh so delicate, octopus. I lie flat on the cold table, the whiteness of the ceiling lights stinging. The machine whirs and beeps and prints out a long dot-matrix page with swooping lines like a repeated signature, the odd timeline of my heart. My nurse tears the sheet off and collects the readout. She tries to gather it all together but the pages unfurl from her grasp spilling to the floor like threads. Suddenly I can read the words, upside down on the bottom of the page, in all caps. It says: *ABNORMAL.*

There it is, in one word. Something really is wrong. I am broken and wrecked. I lay still, trying to absorb that word, I hear my doctor tell the nurse just outside the exam-room door, "He needs to been seen tomorrow. If they can't get him in, you let me know and I will talk to them and make it happen." I sit up, still wired in to this machine that has just called out my heart, just named me precarious. The world collapses beneath me and I am tumbling down a darkened tunnel toward abnormal. There is nothing below me but silence and cold—*the empty, white, blank, unblinking center of it all.*

The next day I arrive at the hospital in a light that is cold and flat and pale under the thin November sun with a delicate wash of snow already sluicing across the asphalt. The grove of white pines beyond the hospital stands dark and empty and only a dead mess of old ferns and bracken—rust-colored and brittle—bristles through the clumped snow at their roots. With one of those ludicrous gowns on, I am strapped down on the table by a sweet man from Haiti, his accent like bougainvillea and the weighty sun. He lays heavy boards across my chest, strapping them down and cinching them across my chest, and feeds me into the cardiac MRI. Into the hole, the giant O of its mind like a mouth, like a cave, like a vortex where soon magnetic fields and pulses of radio waves will thrum down into my chest to paint a portrait of my inner workings. Inches from my face, the ceiling of the tube presses down. I am buried in the mind of this machine. I am tight inside a suit made of science. And then that feeling comes back, like I am inside Suck Hole and the water pounds on me. I am dropped into the cold froth again. I spin and spin in the dark. The water, the nowhere. The machine whirs and bangs. The pressure of it roofs me and there is nowhere to go.

I lie still and panic. I close my eyes and try to breathe but the boards strapped across my chest hold me down. I don't want to open my eyes because there it will be, the roof descending, closing down on me. One quick breath. The machine spins and spins its bulky lens around me, the bang and whack and thrum—so loud!—of the scan's radiation rushing through me. My legs want to kick, hard, like a swimmer deep down striving up toward the light, pushing up into the air, but I stay still. I have to. I need to know. The weight of the boards strapped across my chest spreads like poured sand. The weight of it all compressing me, shoving me down into a shoebox, a tiny tin filled with breath alone. That's all I am, all I have left, those quick breaths. I can breathe in the dark. The banging whang of the machine echoes, but I stay still and breathe.

Slower and slower. Each breath the proof that the next will come. I take slow breaths in the dark as the machine hums and groans around me in the immaculately white room.

§

Keats' bird-not-born-for-death who inhabits this idyllic space of flowers and full-throated summer, the permanent ease of fecund nature, this wild-Costa-Rica of an animal, is both a representative of an unobtainable world of perfection and grandeur and a reminder to Keats of the world of fever and of fret in which he lives—the world of his father's death and his mother's consumption. The world where he and his brother will die within the year. The nightingale represents all that is not human (us with our layers of history and grief and sorrow); it sings a song of ease and light that is not echoed in this, the broken world. Despite the rational fact that this is a mortal bird (I assume it dies like everything else), its song and kind have lived time beyond years and sung for the emperor and clown and even for *the sad heart of Ruth, when, sick for home, She stood in tears amid the alien corn.* When Keats asks for the nightingale's immortal pastoral power to let him slip the bonds of muddled earth and human life, *Where but to think is to be full of sorrow,* he is refused and returned, hard, to his solitary and isolated being.

> *Forlorn! the very word is like a bell*
> *To toll me back from thee to my sole self!*

For the human world, that kind of permanence—those *faery lands*—is unattainable. It is *forlorn*, as Keats says, and the etymology of that word brings us back to loss. The word comes from Old English, past participle of *forlēosan*, to lose. Keats is *lost.* He catches himself using the unbearable gong of that word, hears himself saying it—*forlorn!*—and like a tolling bell it returns him to the human world. To name that place, to call them *faery lands forlorn* both calls them into being through the magic of language—the human version of the bird's song—and breaks the spell, causing him to lose the dream, and returns him to the human world. Because words work in both ways. This is the electricity of both. The metaphor of the poet's song both evokes the enchanted, perfect world beyond the walls of the city *and* denies us access. Even though we can name it, such perfection was never ours.

The song of the nightingale is the elegant cacophony of the natural world, that world so rich in detail and profusion—its productivity and diversity driven by evolution and the dynamic engine of death. By comparison the poet is blind, in a sense, and can only guess at the world's particulars. Keats cannot see the flowers that are at his feet. He cannot, equally, say what this perfect pastoral of the nightingale means or of what exactly it is made. There exist only guesses in the human world. The bird vanishes, withdraws, until it is buried deep in the distant possible wealth of the idyllic pastoral, and the poet is left speculating about his powers in the face of this absence: *Fled is that music:—Do I wake or sleep?* Does language posses the power of the bird? He asks. Is there anything that can cross the boundary between ourselves and the world? Are words that tool, and do they work? Or are we just kidding ourselves? These are my questions. Keats just says it better.

These *faery lands forlorn*, they are what I have been running off to every winter—in the face of the sluicing snow and the black-and-white monotone of the winter fields in Maine where I live now. The eternal green of a landscape that my thoughts return to, imagine, recreate, and resemble. This shining Costa Rica in my mind where the world lives out its perpetual, verdant youth. This land of impossible birds, this rough beach named for the turtles who drop their eggs into shallow holes where they gleam like dirty pearls, this vast city of ants lit by the light of their own unending labor, this architecture of the misted woods and the *chir-roop* of the quetzal echoing off towered fig trees. It was always gone, just as it was spoken into being, faded off beyond the hills and away. That world exists and recedes from us, from me. It is birdcall, silenced as I pass, song returning slowly, and with great caution as I move away. Like the quetzal it flows up the hillsides away from my presence. If we manipulate experience and place through language—and clearly that is what I think we do—then even when I am there I am not there. Our lives are at odds with our very desires. We are broken and frail. I am broken. I am frail. We are (I am) left alone with death.

One way or another, the body turns against itself; we are damaged and we die. That's the truth that Keats tells us, him and his damned bird. This is the truth of elegy and biology alike. Our spoken language and our genetic language, they tell the same story. Mutations drive evolution—the environment acting on the rough wood of the species—but often, too often, these changes, these little fragments of happenstance, do not push a species forward. They are, after all, false steps: error, inaccuracy, and misstep. They are miscommunication and breakdown. They are loss and illogic in the dialogue of the self. Occasionally error finds itself thriving, turned useful in the great gamble of time, but more often than not, error means only death. And just as our language holds fossils—static pieces of meaning and insight that no longer sing their full relationship to the natural world—so too does our very DNA. Our DNA contains fragments and pieces of ancient gestures and tasks (encoding proteins, turning cellular growth on and off, etc.) inside its looping staircase. They work mostly for our benefit, but occasionally and terrifyingly, they turn against us, turn into a distorted version of our normal selves. We know what happens when words turn against us. We have in the 21st Century, at the very least, been taught this lesson: when the power of language—and metaphor— is used to hide horror from our own consciousness, when a *final solution* is defined to conceal genocide. When we screen from sight, in a new language of pain, those so precisely ransacked in the civil service of torture, adding only decoration to the *interrogation* when we *enhance* it like an arabesque stitching to the border of a shroud. But our bodies—our underlying codes—they are a mystery unto us.

We are fragile creatures in a fragile world, connected to the larger places we inhabit by language and story and metaphor. But such connections are fragile too; our stories are often lies, our metaphors weak, broken, and insubstantial in the face of nature's constant flux. We can never know enough, and nature spins away again on its axis. We simplify complication and regulate intricacy. Our desire for understanding and comprehension, our desire for safety or simple comfort pushes us away from the wealth and complexity of the natural world. Cities are the apotheosis of this division, the way they represent the wild in garden and house and lawn, the way they attempt to articulate in building and road what the world resembles, but with safety and with comfort and ease. So it seems that cities are not, in fact, the opposite of the pastoral; they are in some ways its fullest representation. The city carves space out of raw nature for us, a place where we can feel safe and at home. The house stands like an ancient cave or castle (we've heard those metaphors before) with its lawn spread out like the field of welcome where the shepherds graze. The apartment up in the sky like a hole carved in a tree where the quetzal lives its magnificent life. And in those gestures the city streamlines the complexity of the natural world and simplifies its threats. The simplicity of the city is our choice. The natural world, in its complexity and danger, is too large, too intricate, too extensive even in its smallest gestures, and so the village becomes our home in a way that wild nature can no longer be because we are not made for complexity, or for permanence.

§

The man who performed that blessing for us up that small river in a tiny reserve in the Amazon, that man was one of the last speakers of his language. He lived his life in the twilight of the rainforest, between the thriving complexity of the natural world and the simplicity of the city. He learned the names of the plants and their stories; he knew the weather and the slender churning of the fishes. He knew the stealth and quiet of the mammals. He knew the history of the water flowing down from the distant snows of the Andes, the way the river rose and fell each year like a year-long tide. He lived, too, in a space between his language and its isolation. And a linguistic extinction parallels the biological one that is happening across the globe. Although the number of languages spoken in the world is unknown (it is estimated at a bit less than 7,000), 60 – 80% of these languages can be classified as endangered, meaning that children will not be speaking them in 100 years. This extinction is caused by modernity and a collective consumerism that drives us towards uniformity and the calming monopolies of English, Arabic, Spanish, and Mandarin.

He spoke his fragile language. He kept it alive for a year or two more. He stayed behind while the others floated off down the rivers to the floating slums outside of Iquitos, the Barrio de Belén. Thatched shacks stacked on floating rafts and bridged with boats. Water-labyrinth of hovel and lean-to, of pier and piling, of transient history and migration floating on a slow, green lagoon connected to the Amazon River. Even his sons, he told us, left to find an easier life. He stayed behind and kept up the ritual, did the hard work that kept the language alive for another day, because he was one of the last ones, he said, because he had to. As we left the clearing and walked down to the boats, he stood alone on the pounded earth; he stood alone, then he stooped down, re-entered the curve of the palm hut, and disappeared.

§

He walks in and fills the small exam room. Its sparkling whiteness, its sterility filled with his presence. Tall with dark, short curls and a powerful face. I stand to greet him. Weeks later, after the initial hospital visit, I have traveled to Boston from Maine to see this man, this specialist. This cardiac specialist. I expect a serious man with a quiet, expert demeanor.

"Good to meet you," he barks.

I stand and reach out my hand and he takes it in a strong arm, flips our hands up, and pulls me into a bro hug, chests bumping behind our crossed arms. Taken aback, I sputter out, "You, too—" before he moves to sit across from me.

"I've looked at your echo and your MRI," he says. "How'd that go, by the way?"

"Like being buried alive." I shudder.

He chuckles. Deep and throaty. I think my answer was expected.

I talk about my symptoms—the blackouts and the pain running ribbons down my side and around my diaphragm. I talk about walking up stairs, how difficult that has become, how embarrassing it is to arrive at the top of a small flight of stairs heaving and gasping as if I had sprinted up ten flights. I talk about my medications.

He then turns to the computer on the desk, clicks, and pulls up several grainy images, blobs of white and black filling the screen and scrimmed with numbers and words, covered in an unspoken code. The image there, a white bulge filling the dark and grainy space, looks like the sonogram photos where I saw the first images of my son so many years ago.

"Well, the good news is I know what's wrong," he says. "You can see it here."

He points to an image on the monitor, a band of white fuzz on a black field like half an inverted pear. "The septum of your heart is enlarged and each time your heart beats, the bulk of the septum blocks up the left ventricle and obstructs the flow of blood out through the aorta. So, like when you put your thumb over a garden hose, the water comes out faster, harder right? Same here; your blood shoots out with too great a force—that's what causing the pain in your chest and down your left side—but the blood also backs up, through the chambers of your heart and into your lungs. That's what's causing your blackouts. That's the pressure. That's why you can't breathe."

He looks at me evenly. The power of his gaze is dramatic and steady. But I am crumbling. The world is wrong. No, I am wrong. I am uneven and broken. My heart is abnormal.

"Now this isn't something you did, or didn't do. It's genetic. Normal muscle fibers run with each other." He laces the fingers on both hands together. "See? Smooth and flat. But for you, the muscle fibers cross each other." He rotates his hands so the fingers come together at perpendicular angles. "See how they bunch up and jam? That's what's happening here in your heart. The tissue in your septum grows in a cross-hatch and that's what's mucking up the works."

I am silent in the chair, and the room is falling away around me, dropping and dropping. I am broken at a very deep level and it will never get better. My heart is wrong. Even as it beats away inside me I feel it as something other. It is a mutant, a growth, some sort of alien creature in my chest. The floor falls away. The white walls rise to the sky and I sit below them as if at the bottom of the deepest well.

Something is wrong at the core of the instructions that built me; that's what he is saying. I want to feel guilty. To blame myself. Instead, he is telling me the opposite, that in my private language there is, simply, an error. Even in that most fundamental script—the careful equivalence of my genes—there can be slippage. And there it is. Here. In my body. In my heart. Things get misplaced or misworded and some fragment of my DNA is off, by just a little, some slight margin of error, some typo, and that one misspoken word deep in the language I am chained to means things have gone horribly wrong. Diseased, I think, but that's not correct. My heart and its abnormality are part of the same force that drives evolution and speciation. That slight variation in my code, that's what evolutionary pressure acts on, for the strength of the species, if not the individual. This heart, this heart I now see as damaged, as alien, as other, even as it beats inside my chest, is part of the natural world, its muscle and rhythm part of the process of nature, even in its failure. I can't, finally, separate myself from nature, despite my linguistic attempts to do so. Even when the words I use (words like the 21st century version of "nature" that divides the world in half), even when my words drive a wedge between my conscious, linguistic thought and the world outside my mind, even then, the connection is too fundamental and essential to be denied. That enlargement like a sliced pear bulging in the atrium of my heart connects me to the world even as it drags me down.

"Now here's the bad news," he says. "That fatigue, that pain: they are here to stay. And there is a very real potential for cardiac arrest. The arteries that feed the heart branch first from the aorta, right?" He draws a brief sketch of the heart on a sheet of paper on the desk and points to two branching arteries coming off the aorta just outside the heart. "And when they don't receive the blood they need, because of that aortic obstruction we talked about, the heart pumps harder to compensate, depriving itself in a feedback loop..." He doesn't need to finish the sentence. I get it. Heart failure. Death.

"But, you have options," he continues. "There is medication. And there is surgery." But I am on the medication already—a beta-blocker. It was the first thing they gave me in the GP's office, before anyone knew what was happening, before anything was certain. This medication slows the beat of my heart, regulates the muscle, and keeps my heart from going into overdrive. This medication keeps my heart from entering that terrible feedback loop, keeps me alive. It sucks—not to put too fine a word to it. I am constantly exhausted. I sleep eleven hours a night and nap every day. My blood has been replaced with cold molasses. And this is on the lowest dose. As my condition worsens—as it will, he says—I will need to up the dosage to keep pace. And it is forever. I will never be able to stop taking it. Every day is harder. Every day I am more exhausted. Every day those single flights of stairs seem to rise taller and taller before me. Every day my chest aches more.

"The other choice is surgery," he says. "Cardiac surgery. We will enter the left ventricle through the aorta and we will *simply*"—that's the word I hear him say, *simply*—"excise the enlargement and relieve the symptoms." The language he uses is careful and controlled. I recognize it. The language of science and certainty.

"Take your time," he says. "Think about it." *As if I wasn't.* "Let us know what you want."

I know what I want. I want to walk out into the green world, to run and never stop. *Solvitor ambulando.* I want to take back my life, my youth, and my body. I want to run back to that wild beach in Costa Rica, to watch the pelicans cross the glass surf on mysterious errands all their own. I want to stand beneath an almond tree decorated with a festival of scarlet macaws. I want the elegant buzz of a green violetear humming in the rain-wet air. I want sunlight mottling the perfect trails of the leaf-cutter ant. I want a quetzal accessorizing the fig tree above the velvet of the Savegre River at dusk. I want beauty uncomplicated by human presence. I want raw and uncomplicated nature, but there is no such thing. I want to hide in a world devoid of people and empty of my broken body.

But that can't happen. I am nature, my heart is a part of the world, and it is (we are) (I am) fragile.

I walk from the hospital beneath the noon sun, cold and unwarm through a gray swirl of clouds, all alone. I have hours to wait until my bus leaves for Maine and nowhere to go. Usually I love the anonymity of the city, the possibilities that spread from wandering for hours through new streets and the brownstones, the café at the corner with the small cups of espresso like tea sets, perhaps a glass of Syrah, deep ruby like the color of dried blood, and then out to the river where the gulls scoot down toward the harbor and return. The city hums and hisses. The cold belching of exhaust all around me. People in black and blue with small splashes of red (the uniform of Boston during football season). The cold sunlight of late autumn. I could walk the Common and across, down to the Charles and look for ducks. I could wander Chinatown and its maze of alleys and dim sum. Instead I hollow out the rest of the day in a basement bar—like a low-rent Cheers!—beneath neon lights and cold shadows in every corner. I drink and drink in the dim dim forever-dim twilight of a bar in daytime. The sentimental gloss of the sunlight outside called so quickly into question by its absence in the dark.

§

Keats had twice hemorrhaged blood from his lungs in February 1820 and by spring his doctors believed that another winter in London would cost him his life. So he abandoned Fanny Brawne, his love, back in London and with longtime friend Joseph Severn, left for Rome in the fall, trying to outrun the tuberculosis that had set up camp in his lungs.

The trip itself was difficult and certainly didn't help. Severe storms wracked his ship, the brig Maria Crowther, and those storms were followed by a dead calm in which the ship could make no progress. Finally docking in Naples, the ship was held in quarantine ten days for fear of cholera. Keats finally arrived in Rome in November of 1820. He hoped the city would save him. Three months later, in a small apartment adjacent to the Spanish Steps, he was dead.

XIII.

In the gray swirl of early winter, a month later, I lie down on a shining bed of wheels and tubing, beneath powerful lights, while nurses and the anesthesiologist loom over me like strange, blue buildings. They chat and question me, try to keep me talking while my eyes well with tears and I say goodbye to Jennifer, my equally weeping wife. Her face is streaky as a rain-wet window, her hair dark and down. I wish I knew what to say. I want to comfort her but I am wordless. I am dazed and lost. She can't speak either—her world is askew—and I am damaged and lost to her as if floating away down a river while she watches alone on the rocky shore. Her eyes blue as deep seawater behind her glasses. I look at her and see the weight of a solitary future resting on her shoulders. I am that future; we both know it. In it I am absent and she is alone, alone with our son and the rest of her life. I start to apologize, to ask forgiveness for this failure of mine. For this fragile heart I carry. But she just squeezes my hand. A nurse pulls her away, saying, "Time to go." The nurse looks into my wife's face, now nearly breaking with fear and says, "Oh, don't worry. He's going to be fine. We do this all the time." Then they are both gone. I am on my own.

I lie on the bed looking into the brightness, the inhuman glow of the florescent lights like small boxes of God. Someone sticks a probe up the artery in my arm to monitor my blood pressure and pulse, and multiple IVs in the other. I am attached to a thicket of wires. I am being assimilated. The anesthesiologist is there, above me, happy and jovial, making jokes. Then it is time. He wheels me down corridors of green and weird, as if I'm being funneled down some hallway deep in the bowels of the X-Files. We bang into doorways and twist strange corners. I am heading right toward it—*the empty, white, blank, unblinking center of it all*. It seems impossible at some deep and necessary layer that I can survive this. I have been close many times. You know the stories now, my sad architecture of easy woe. In the cold current of the Six Mile, deep in the Peruvian rainforest bristled with wasps, but those moments all had the blessing of surprise. I never had to walk willfully and carefully up to that gap in the world.

In the days leading up to my surgery I prepared as if for my own funeral. I wept easily and often. As I taught my final class of the semester, guiding the students through the layering of nature and death in Keats, or crossed the field with the dog one last time, the grass bent and sere and burned brown by early winter, the rocks at the edge of the river glazed with ice, the path hard with frost's white iron, each episode felt like the end of a story. I wrote letters to my wife and son to be delivered from beyond the grave. I ate like the condemned—each meal my last. Even though I knew the odds and they were heavily in my favor, I still felt like the dead-man walking. Every part of me wanted to run, to head for the green hills and light out for the territory beyond the horizon where my heart would somehow be reborn. But I stayed on task. I took one step and then another and followed the plan. I moved forward because I had no other option.

If the complexity of nature works against us and rejects our attempts to define it, then these early encounters with death merely stand in for the thing itself. *They resemble.* The road at the top of a mountain descending in every direction into cloud is a metaphor for how lost I am wandering the wide world. The coat of wasps I wore up the Tahuayo argues that I am not welcome in the rainforest, in nature. The cold vortex of the Six Mile stands in for the impossibility of finding any final answers. But here I am now, in this very real and physical city, confronted with the reality of it, the end of my life. But it's not here. The reality, I mean. It is, but it's not. There is no form I can give to this moment of ultimate importance that won't be artificial. No construct that won't be designed to make me appear brave or stoic or perhaps even at peace. But I am none of those things.

I slide down long corridors filled with beds and machines, the lights above counting down as I approach the operating theater. We bang the doors open with my heavy bed-on-wheels and we're in. The room is strikingly cold and bright and filled with noise. Gowned men and women swirl around, manipulating machines and trays of tools. My nurse is above me, smiling behind her mask. I can see it in her eyes. She says something I can't follow. Kind words. Gentle. I am woozy from the meds they have already given me. I am at the end of a long tunnel. They are all far away. The rooms softens, turns to water. And I am gone.

§

If that dark shadow of death hides in plain sight—in the ghostly form swirling inside the cold flux of the Six Mile, in a dark log thrumming with wasps, inside the illusionary stability of the earth, or even in my own beating heart—then perhaps there is a better, more human ground for my investigation of place. The city. Perhaps the city that I tried to reject long ago and failed, this sprawling village we make with our own toil like those leaf-cutter ants laboring in long tunnels lit by the light of their own efforts, maybe some welcome geography out among the foothills of old mountains or an old town ringed by ancient walls, maybe the city is the ground where fragile human gestures of language and art can find solid footing. Maybe the city with its layering of art and history and memory, maybe, as Keats thought, maybe the city can save us.

A city is more comprehensible than the raw material of wild nature from which it is constructed; it should be much easier to understand the built environment than the wild. It should be easier to read Paris than the rainforest, easier to understand the fabric of Rome over the texture of the deserts of the American West. Buildings are markers of meaning and sense, laid out by humans for human use, but, as in the natural world, there are layers and layers of meaning and construction inside the simplest locale; and much of the meaning inside any city, in any place, lies in the memories and history it holds. But memory, like language, is pliable and the place I call home now sounds like leaving.

This town I left to come here, to this hospital, to this operating theater. This town, I need to think more clearly about it. Not the town so much as the place— Western Maine. The mountains in Maine where people hold on in the dark corner of winter to a life that must have seemed rich and possible 200 years ago when the pine forests were flowing down the river to the sea and the land blossomed with the farms and opened land. Today, trees rise up through abandoned farmland, and stone walls and foundations of old homesteads haunt the hidden corners and back roads. My town itself is small and thriving, a little oasis in a landscape of once and ghost. Farmington. The name itself conjures up hope and progress, green fields marked out along the river valleys by tree breaks and stone fences pulled from the earth itself, a wet wind coming out of the south that meant rain. Then a sweet taste must have remained on all the lips, like an uncommon fog or perfume off a woman's neck. But today, the landscape of Western Maine is defined by decline—young people leave and don't return. The factories and mills have, for the most part, gone south. And yet my town holds on— and does much better than many of our neighbors, it must be said. Still the wind sounds like leaving.

§

In the ICU my first thought is, *I woke up*. With my eyes still sewn shut by the drugs, I come back to the world, to its sounds and the feel of my body in the dark as if exiting a long, long tunnel. *I woke up.* The act alone feels monumental. I am still groggy and my brain is full of a heavy mist, but I am alive. My eyes struggle against their own weight but at the edges of their blackout-darkness a light creeps in. I feel and hear the nurse leaning over me, gruff and shouting, "I need you to squeeze my hands. I need you to hear me!" In the darkness I reach up and grab her hands like a swimmer reaching for the ladder, coming up out of deep water and desperate for air. I squeeze with all the strength I have. I float up into the mundane room where I lie, the drop ceiling above me slightly stained, the cabinets and the machines surrounding me like concerned friends. I wake with Christmas music burbling from the radio and the TV above my bed blazing Fox News like some form of punishment I am not sure I deserve. My chest aches like a box of pain and I am wired up and down. The chatter of the machines speaks one story about my recovery, but it feels like another story inside my own body. I was broken apart and reassembled. I can feel the seams in me, and my heart pounds so hard I rock, ever so slightly, back and forth in the bed. Still, I am past it—and never has the mere fact of consciousness felt so glorious.

I am awake and I want my life back in all its grubby necessity. I want out of this bed. More than anything, I want to stand up and walk out into the sloppy Boston December with all its complication and noise—the hiss of exhaust trailing from traffic, the jangle of Chinese on the restaurant marquees, dirty snow clumped against the trees all across the Common.

§

In my home in Western Maine, the streets of the towns blow with sand and smell of soap and sulfur. Many days, the wind carries the smell of the last remaining paper mill that blows clouds into the low sky and for years dumped poison into the rivers. Cars swing their wide turns at random. And the people leave. They move, packing everything in small, flat boxes, hauling bicycles and cars, mattresses strapped to the roofs of their cars like airfoils. Even if they don't, they spend hours imagining leaving. They plan and scheme, envisioning new lives in towns far distant, towns that carry the smell of exhaust, towns where the air holds the salt of the sea, towns with staggering skyline. They imagine new jobs, positions of authority, deal-making and posturing. They call the Chambers of Commerce in these places, just in case.

I have reversed course—moving against the drift of people and their belongings, making my home out here in a city in the foothills where the wind begins, where the snow piles up against fences and the sky is quiet. I have come for a job I like well enough, teaching creative writing and literature to students whose dream is to be anywhere but here, to students who blink and shake their heads when asked if they ever consider staying around after graduation, who want out to cites like Portland and Boston. I have been to the places my students dream of going. I have lived in Pittsburgh and Washington and Colorado. I have lived in the mountains and by the sea. I have walked out of my door into an alley behind a dry cleaner, scurried through the underground subways and tunnels, and bopped from club to club all night. I have opened my porch into a deer-rich pasture below a 12,000 foot mountain, the early morning light catching the edges of the peak like a thumbnail moon. I have been a few other places, too.

When Elizabeth Bishop asks whether we should have just damn well stayed at home and tended to the tiny gardens of our own lives, she means her question to cut through the easy rhetoric of place. She knows the question is necessary and the answer obvious, but she asks it regardless. Because still she goes; she makes her loop from Key West to Boston, losing something from each locale each time. She abandons Nova Scotia and returns to it only in memory. She stays in Brazil and loses Maine. I believe that there is an explicit good to traveling and seeing the world not designed for me. But there is a cost to our voyaging, clearly, as Bishop teaches us in her work. We are not saved by lighting out for the territory ahead of all the rest; we are not healed simply by setting out again for a new horizon. All our problems—they are not solved by walking. Yet still I go. This is the Alaskan in me, the Californian. It is the immigrant and the expatriate in me. It is the Roma in me, the traveler. It is the Muir in me, the Kerouac, the Appleseed. This is the ancient African in me who first put heel to toe and left that long Rift Valley full of sunlight and gazelles and walked into a new world. It is the American in me, thinking that novelty teaches and enriches us. That it *is* ultimately worth the while to go round the world to count the cats in Zanzibar.

§

In the ICU, the sun pounds off the skyscrapers outside the window and the sky buzzes blue as two oceans woven together. The TV flashes and jumps; monitors chatter with blips and information from my wired body—but I cannot speak. I am alive. I am alive, but when I try to articulate this very important and necessary fact, I can't say a word. The tube down my throat, the intubation tube for the ventilator that kept me alive during surgery, is still in place. My throat stiff and solid, my head back. I reach for it, for my mouth—woozily—and I miss. The drugs in my system still course their way across the broad delta of my brain. I am all afuzz. The nurse pins my hands to the bed, hard, her strength remarkable, and yells, "We need to leave that in for 30 minutes! We need to know that you can breathe on your own!"

I lie back and can feel every inch of that tube filling my throat, my thin breath slipping out through a hole at the top like I am breathing out a chimney. My throat is packed and full, my chest as solid as steel. I am trapped inside a box made of my own body and only a filament of air connects me to the world. I close my eyes again and I am at the bottom of a tunnel breathing up into a far distant sky. My throat choked, as if with ash, as if with mud. Thirty minutes. I am going to sink back into myself before that. My throat is dammed up. I want to rip it out, that blockage, but I have no strength. I am in deep water, with only that long filament of hose connecting me to the surface, to my world. I am drowning inside the bed, the machines rising up around me like a forest of kelp. I shiver and shake, as if with a bone-deep cold, and my nurse piles blankets across me. She is counting down. Twenty minutes. I lie still and count my thin breath.

Fifteen minutes.

With each breath, I shove the air to the surface, out that tube that fills me; that tube has now has taken over my whole body until all that I am is blocked by it, and then I extract a thread of fresh air from the hollowness at my core. I hold on to that slender bridge, that narrow reed that reaches up into the light. My chest aches and stiffens. I lie still and strain with every muscle. Every piece of me wants to climb the ladder of that tube and clamber into the world that lies just beyond me, but I can't move. I am drowning inside my own body.

Ten minutes.

I shake and shake. "You're so cold," the nurse says and lays another blanket across my legs. But I am not. I am falling away from the room, falling down and down into that hole in my throat, into my own body, a hole like a diamond made of darkness that draws everything down into it, a black hole, a vortex, the current of my own breath pulling me deeper and deeper. Down, down, forever down, each breath like a rung deeper, a moss-dark step on some stairway of infinite shadow. I am lost, looking up, trying to hold on to the tiny slice of light that hovers above me like a distant doorway.

Then it is time.

"Breathe out. Breathe! Hard! Hard as you can!"

I exhale, hard, and the nurse pulls that tube from my mouth like a thin accordion, like a magician's trick, yanking the impossibly long line from my stunned and surprised mouth like a train of gaudy handkerchiefs. Suddenly, the darkness is revealed as the illusion, the trick. It vanishes. I am back in the light and the world. When that tube finally comes out of me, I suck a cold, reedy lungful of air into my aching chest and croak, *Let's never do that again.*

§

In the very early morning, the next day after my surgery, in the cardiac ICU, I move from the bed to a chair. Or am moved, lifted physically like a sack of wheat and placed in a hard, Naugahyde recliner where

I promptly fall asleep. The night was hard. The ache and stiffness—like they had implanted a steel plate inside my chest—made it almost impossible to sleep and the fact that my lungs flattened when my heart was stopped meant that my breathing was shallow and thin. The merest wisp of breath. Many of the small pockets and caverns of alveoli in my lungs were still sealed and would take a while to reopen. So, when I lay back on the bed, I heaved and wheezed, and shifting my weight from side to side meant agony. All night I lay inside a painful cage made of my own body and sipped air.

Still in the chair, I wake to a blue sky beyond the windows, a deep, steel blue like the cleanest seawater, and the bright winter sun pounding off the golden skyscraper across town. The sunlight reflects off that building and comes bright and focused into the room. It hits me square in the face with a powerful, focused warmth. The light is blindingly painful in my eyes, but it feels like life, like the life that lives outside this room packed full of beeping and stainless steel. It is everything I want. The nurse comes in, notices I am awake, and says, generously, "Oh, I'll just shut those blinds for you."

"No!" My answer is as much of a shout as I can muster.

"No?" She is shocked. Unsure.

"Please, no. Just leave it."

I can't explain it to her, how much I need that light and warmth pouring over me. It means the world outside the room is still there. That sounds obvious, I know. But the world feels new to me, like it is reborn with me. The death I felt coming was not only my own; it was the world's death as well. It was the absence of the world and its loss that I feared as much as my own death. It was nothingness. I have no faith in anything beyond this world—I believe in art and I believe in language and I believe in love but there is no sky kingdom waiting for me when I die—and most days that is a comfort and a blessing and gives meaning and intensity to everything I do. But when confronted with the absolute absence of my mind in the world, my thinking falters.

I sit in that same chair all day. Literally. I don't move from that spot. I can't. I am tied down with catheters and the chest tubes draining the pink, bloodstained fluid from deep within my body. But I watch the sun cross the blue sky. I watch the small ballet of a few clouds drift in off the ocean. I can see a world, just a piece of a world really, a messy and occasionally painful landscape I desperately want. People come and go, my wife and my mother, their eyes tired and brimming with relief. The machines beep and hum, but the sky stays blue for a long time, until late afternoon when it slowly loses its light and falls to darkness.

§

I want to get back to it, to understand what it means, but once again I can only get so close to it—the center of my life where my life, in fact, ends. I can approach it but finally it veers away and I am left alone with my images. There I am in my imagined scene, floating above myself like a cheap Hollywood phantasm. The doctors stand blue and sphinxlike in their bundled layers, the nurses and techs alive and busily severe in the frigid operating theater. My chest stretched open like a clam-can. Like an open zipper. Like a tunnel descending into the earth. How to describe it? The doctors and nurses, the PAs, they swirl around me and this huge wound in my chest, this dark and still center. They approach it closer than I can. Their experience of my heart is real and concrete and physical—it is bloody and marled with fat like a fine steak iced down for freshness (seriously—they packed my heart in ice during the procedure).

But for me this moment stands like an impossible eddy at the center of my life. Maybe there are no words for my experience of it. Perhaps I need to turn absence into presence through metaphor because I cannot evoke it on its own. It is the unsayable. I imagine the hole in my chest like Escher's two hands drawing each other, that diamond of space between them pulled open by the act of creation itself. The two hands pencil each other into being, but in doing so they must pull away from each other. The space between those hands—shadowed and stretched by their very efforts at creating one another—defines them. My chest lies open and dark, its insides visible—that unblinking center of my life, that eye of the hurricane, that peak surrounded by clouds, that vortex churning inside me—and the doctors ladder down into my body to excavate the piece that has gone wrong. They climb down and down into my open chest braced by the rib-spreader like the mouth of a mine shaft where at the bottom lies my still and unbeating heart.

XIV.

Twenty years ago in a June like this one—gray and grizzled with rain and the low clouds that enamor the north part of the continent in early summer—I first flew to Europe. And now, twenty years later I am back. After my surgery, after my recovery, my chest sewn together and wired shut, the bones fused again and a white-purple seam running down my chest, I am back. I want to go back to the past and wallow in memory, to show my son a world I wandered through long ago. For him, I want a world bigger than the boundaries of our small town in Maine. I want to show him the width of the world. But we land in an airport where little has changed. There are flat screen TVs, Wi-Fi, but an airport waiting lounge is an airport waiting lounge— anonymous by design.

Back then I had a friend with me, Tony, another twenty-three year old looking to avoid the realities of post-graduate life for a while. Tony was a gangle of limbs, a scarecrow of a boy-becoming-a-man, and I was little different. He worked construction for six months to earn the $6,000 we needed; I waited tables at the Museum Café in St. Louis with a group of flamboyantly gay men who were convinced I was closeted (why else would I work there, in an *art* museum?) and an over-sexed manager who kept trying to get me into bed. Tony and I would spend the next three months together, hopping trains, eating one meal a day to afford beer, jumping back and forth between big cities and small beach towns—my long hair bleached almost platinum from the salt and the sun by the time we left for home from Athens.

We began in Paris, Tony and I, and I vividly remember the city, the flat pan of the sand in the *Jardin des Tuileries* beaten hard with the tramping of thousands of feet, a small café off *Rue du Four* near the Church of Saint-Sulpice where I ate steak *au poivre* and had my first cappuccino, ever, the *tabacs* and the *fromageries* (the smell rich as the angels' feet, as the old line goes) near our hostel, the wind and the sky and the gold-gray expanse of the city laid out around me. But by the time we zigzagged our way across the continent and arrived in Rome, it was late August, blazing with a heat like a thousand smacking hands and the city was emptied of its locals and in their place were too many tourists. (We called ourselves travelers, then, the ones who spent months wandering, and felt far superior to those Americans on their one week bus jaunts running the gauntlet of three or four cities in eight days. Our naiveté is kind of charming now, from this distance.)

But there is a bigger problem. Now, my memories blur and fade. I can see a few clearly: the Sistine Chapel, dank and crowded and packed with too many people; Bernini's piazza, the welcome space of it under the hard light; and the Forum, packed with so much history it was ultimately blank, devoid of meaning. But the details of that time are gone. I have no idea where we stayed, no sense of whom we spoke to, what we ate, or where. Rome is a short slide show of monuments, while Paris is a rich film with full color and dialogue.

Graffiti's hieroglyphics dot most of the buildings and run the train lines that flow into Paris today, through the grit and decay of the suburbs. We are in the train from Charles de Gaulle, watching the City of Lights accumulate in the early morning fog of jet lag. Paris reverses the American model in many ways; people want to live in the city center and pay handsomely to do so, so the poor live on the fringes and they make their mark. Paris, as we arrive at the *Gare du Nord*, feels as modern as it ought to—iPads, Wi-Fi, cellphones, this traffic of smart cars and bike shares—it feels urban. But at its heart there is also something deeply traditional (not ancient, but traditional) about Paris. It lives on in the pastoral dream of old France, evoked in the markets on *Rue Cler* where we are staying—a small stretch of road, blocked off for pedestrians and echoing the patterned landscape, the plastered pastel farmhouses and small towns around tree-break roads and the old canals now thick with poplar and elm. It evokes the village that the city once was, that allegorical village where most of our lives as humans have been spent, in France or Nigeria or India or China. It seems we are villagers at heart and in our stories, and the village—the heart of the city—is where our minds return to when allowed.

I write all this in my journal in Café Roussillon, drinking espresso and savoring the flow of the street around me: *Rue Cler* and its pastiche of markets, the *fromagerie*, and the grocer with his shelves of blackberries and nectarines and flowers like the palette-board of an oil painter dabbled and smeared with vermillion, cobalt, and ochre. I write while my wife and son sleep off their jet lag in the flat we have rented just up *Rue Saint-Dominique,* the shades pulled down deep into an almost damp darkness. I have been thinking a long time about place, about the *where of things,* but for me that *where* has long been defined by wildness, by the absence and distance of human life, by the raw material of the natural world. But like Keats, I have turned to the city now. I have turned to the city looking for a way to define the world where I spend most of my time and a way to understand how language can create the necessary architecture of meaning that might be able to articulate the way I want to live and why and where.

Language and the city—it seems to me—are not the same, but they are similar. They are human-built, systems of signs designed for consumption. Each presents an image of solidity and permanence. And each is readable. The stark, black words on the page. The physical actuality of the Church of Saint-Julien-le-Pauvre in the early light. But each changes, of course. Places change with the day-to-day alterations of light and leaf, with the unhurried swing of each season as it passes, the gargantuan slowness of the mountain giving way and descending into the plain. So, too, does language change as it ages; we add new words and read old ones in new ways. We add depth and knowledge to the layers of meaning each word represents. Some fall away, abandoned, while others are revealed anew by the wearing of time and custom.

The enterprise of meaning created from the raw storehouse of language and the city built out of the unprocessed matter of the wild: each represents a kind of desire in the world, a desire for durability and denotation, a desire for meaning and communication, for finality and truth, for permanence. We build each and we should be able to read each. We inscribe the meanings we extract from their cores in fresh, new ways, in articulations of sound and sense, but—and here's the crux—both place and word ultimately fail to sustain that permanence and each survives only as a kind of memory.

And so, in some ways, this second trip to Europe is about memory; it is an attempt to make up for the words I didn't write twenty years ago, the images and moments I didn't record that are now lost because I believed I would remember it all in my youthful vanity, but of course we all lose by degrees every day the worlds that we inhabit in our minds. We build certain scenes from the rubble and defend them as if they were true and real and accurate, as if they were honest and correct, but they are constructions. And the act of building one thing means others vanish, torn down to make way for this work. Our minds work the way cities work—patches of the past remain as the old world is torn down daily to make room for the new. The space where something once lived, a story or a building, is now repurposed and renovated, created anew out of the fragments of the past, the way Rome was built from the ruins of the ancient world, the way renovated Paris rose from the limestone quarries beneath the meadows that once circled the town, those long labyrinths then filled up with millions of bones from the emptied graveyards of the old city.

§

In the *Bar du Central* down the street where we eat the first evening (a small family brasserie, classically Parisian, back and white tile, noisy and well-lit, *croque madame, escargot, steak frites*), our waiter switches almost effortlessly into English after my rusted attempts to order in French clatter around his feet. This will happen again and again in Paris, this unforced and graceful linguistic two-step that was not present twenty years ago (but my French was much better then, too). Twenty years ago, I made my way through the linguistic barricades of Paris while my friend, who spoke Spanish but no French, felt scorned and beaten down in every store and bar we went in. Famously, in France, the

Académie française has long sought to protect the purity of the French language from creeping Americanization by English-language media and culture. The *Académie's* forty members, known as immortals (seriously), act as an official authority on the language and have tried to prevent English words like *le weekend, le email* and *la software* from being adopted by French users. They have failed.

As the regulars at *Bar du Central*, six or eight men sitting raucously around a table in the back, laugh at Jennifer and mutter *Américaine* with a kind of raucous joy when she misses the labeled door to the bathroom and steps instead into the alley, the memory of another meal in another *brasserie* rises up. The dark interior lit by a few candles and the light behind the bar sparkling on the bottles and in the smoked and crackled mirror. The *steak au poivre* and the carafe of good, nameless local wine, the cappuccino. The sense of good food, not great, but good food done carefully and well. We had no guidebook, no one to help us, Tony and me. We just sat down at a table in a comfortable spot designed for the people of the neighborhood—not for us, although we were welcomed carefully and with courtesy—and that made all the difference. I still remember the steak, medium rare and rich with cracked pepper, the brandy sauce tangy and spiced with honey-like sweetness, the twice-fried *frites, très parisienne,* and the surprising weight of the wine like meat on our tongues.

From the top of the Eiffel Tower the next day, Paris spreads out before us like the perfection of memory. Like mountains, there are some things in the human world that change so slowly that they appear immortal. Here, atop the tower, it could be twenty years ago, easily. Today it is the same parabolic curve of the columns, the same swarm of people crowding the base and the footings. I could be twenty-three again, easily, looking up into the mottle of the Parisian sky for the first time. But, even back then, I had seen the tower so many times, in so many places. Spiking the sky, it was a consistent image, an obvious emblem (so of course it was our first stop—it's a cliché I know, but my son simply *insisted*). Many monuments, and many places, seen too often in advertisements and in film, have become commonplace through the sheer ubiquity of their reproduction. They seem small and fundamentally uninteresting when actually viewed in person. Places and landscapes, like works of art, are lost through reproduction and repetition—the essential qualities of modern, commercial culture—they are diminished and reduced to cliché by their very frequency, their ubiquity representing the fact that they are for sale. The Mona Lisa, for instance, thronged by tourists in the Louvre whose camera flashes bang off its protective glass, small and strangely unimpressive in its gallery off the *Pavillon Denon*. Or Manuel Antonio National Park in Costa Rica reduced to a postcard image of green-fringed islands against the setting sun by the weight of the tourism it carries.

But in person the Eiffel Tower seems almost immune to such depreciation. Almost. Even with its overrepresentation in posters and kitsch (hawkers selling 1 euro replicas, the retro postcard of the tower-in-sepia that line kiosks across the city). While its image is for sale, its actual wrought iron presence looms over Paris and *le Champ de Mars* like some steampunk fantasy, baroque and almost perfectly misplaced in the smooth, low cityscape of Paris. Perhaps because Paris is so low-set, perhaps because the city reclines and simmers around it, perhaps because when approaching it on foot through the seventh *arrondissement* the graceful lunge of the iron surprises from between the trees and, suddenly, there it is; the Eiffel Tower doesn't disappoint. It doesn't disappoint because, despite its strangeness, it seems perfectly in place and looms, in fact, larger in life than it does in reproduction. In other words, sometimes place matters.

To stand beneath the columns looking up at the superstructure, to climb up inside it is to exist outside reproduction. To stand inside the work is to participate in it. The Tower seems to exist outside of time, in a sense, outside of memory's fickle alterations. The tower's late Victorian ethos brought whole into the twenty-first century. The open architecture, the size and scope, the sense of space and the wind beneath the foaming clouds, the fawn and charcoal of the city concentrically ringing out from the Louvre and the *Jardin des Tuileries*, surrounded by the newer shine of the commercial and financial districts. In person, but only in person, there on the *Champs de Mars*, only *there* is it *undiminished* and my son, his hands on a charcoal beam and his voice rough with astonishment, says, "I am touching the Eiffel Tower!"

§

Weeks later, my son and I stand beneath the sign, *Arrête—C'est ici L'Empire de la Mort*, and then, like Dante and a twelve year old Virgil, we drop down into hell. On our last day, beneath massive stone lions in the median and the swirl of traffic about Montparnasse, the stairs drop and drop and in the middle of the journey of my life I descend and again descend in a double helix like the DNA of narrative itself, turning and turning in the narrowing spiral. The story always returns where it began. This story of the accumulation of death below Paris, this chronicle of the catacombs, it starts with placards detailing the technique of the excavation itself, how the city beneath the city was constructed and these tunnels emptied and the stone raised from beneath the surrounding fields to build the elegance of the City of Lights above.

The story builds to bones piled like city walls topped with skulls, long fencing of bone after bone, bones and the green felt of that moss that now gentles the faces of the citizens of these carved cities beneath our feet. The cemeteries were emptied in the old town and all the bones carted here—six million bones—and stored in the long tunnels beneath Paris. That's amazing enough. But a group of tunnel workers—in a monument to their comrades lost to a cave-in like a sudden folding of hands after a day of long labor, lost beneath the sudden collapse of the stone that feels so solid above our heads even now—these workers carved a façade of the *Quartier de Cazerne* into an alcove of one shaft. Amidst this story of loss and death and the creation of a city built from the tunneled excavation deep beneath itself, these men carved a classic portico and the scalloped archways of their home out of the tunnel's wall itself, like the castle of the poets Dante found in hell—those seven gates and beyond, a meadow, fresh and green.

Finished with our tour of this city of the dead, this perfect, elegant hell, and back in the world above, Julian and I eat a late meal at *Au Bouquet* in the narrow sunlight that tunnels through the cloud-cover: *vin rouge* and *chocolate chaud*, charcuterie and cheese like the rough fruit of the earth. My son and I. The living floating above the dead as trees muscle up into that stone-worked sky and traffic hums past on *Boulevard Saint-Jacques*.

§

Memory is what ties me to the past, and it is equally the force that creates the past I am tied to. Memory is story and story, at the end, is all I have, so I will continue. Twenty years ago, when this story begins, Rome was so different: the haze and heat and a dull scramble through the Forum and Colosseum, the traffic and the dirt and the accumulated weariness of months of backpacking across Europe, the pile-up of city after city, the way I wanted to be home but didn't at the same time. All this gave me nothing but distaste for Rome, the dirt and the noise of it, the age and sad decay, as if, as Chad Davidson says, Rome were an ancient, giant ashtray.

This time in Rome, twenty years later, my family and I find a quiet hotel in *Trastevere* (literally "beyond the Tiber") with a leafy courtyard of orange trees off a quiet street, *Vicolo del Piede*, so narrow our taxi barely fits through, isolated and yet central enough that we move in and out of the city easily on buses and taxis and on foot. Nearby, *Santa Maria de Trastevere* tolls the time on the quarter hour and we walk winding streets of charcoal stone, past cafés and bars where the shouts and groans of soccer fans watching the World Cup slip into the street. We have a *panetteria*, a cheese shop, and a small farmer's market in the *Piazza di San Cosimato*—onions and eggplant, peppers and zucchini blossoms, cakes of ice layered with squid and fish, boxes of sunflowers—below the ruined tower. We have the Botanical Garden and the piazza with its late afternoon light, golden and thick on the streets of black stone.

This time, Rome's age feels more inviting, too; the recycled landscape makes sense to me in a way that it had not so many years ago. Perhaps because of my own age, or perhaps because I have read so much more and feel prepared to walk into the Pantheon and know I am seeing the rebuilt form of a temple first created by Marcus Agrippa (and to know who he is) and later rebuilt after its destruction by fire by Emperor Hadrian, to walk the Palatine Hill and understand how the pieces fit, how that citadel was designed to appear out of the hillside above the forum to make it seem as if the palace itself arose from the caves of Romulus, where Rome itself emerged when two brothers were suckled by a wolf.

To see ancient Rome become modern is to watch an accumulation of styles, to watch art and memory layered over and over again, like the nacre inside a shell, like the rings of an ancient tree spreading from a sapling source. As in the ancient hippodrome that became the baroque public space to see and be seen, the *Piazza Navona* with the Egyptian obelisk of Emperor Caracalla reinstalled in the square at the top of Bernini's fountain of the four rivers. To read the memory of the city is to see modern apartments built into the residence of the Orsini family that was itself layered on top of the remains of the Theater of Marcellus—the network of arches, corridors, tunnels, and ramps that gave access to the interior normally ornamented with a screen of engaged Greek columns. It is to imagine the Roman Forum at its height, glistening with travertine, the banners and smoke from the Temple of Caesar, strangled corpses rotting on the Gemonian Stairs, and equally to imagine the *campo vaccino*—the cattle field—it became, buried 10 feet deep in mud and ruin, overgrown and grazed with livestock.

To write Rome—to show it in-depth here and with resonance—is to describe it in history as if in life, as if one year is layered over the top of another. It is to see Nike and Roma on the Arch of Titus, built by Domitian in 70 CE to honor Titus's conquest of Jerusalem, and see the Jews being led beneath it as slaves into the city carrying the seven-branched menorah. It is to see the Jews refusing to walk though that arch again until 1948, when Israel was born, and then the Jews of Rome walked backward through the arch as if reversing time. It is to see the Temple of Antoninus and Faustina, its platform of large peperino blocks and columns of cipollino marble (monolithic and more than 17 meters tall) and the entablature decorated with a frieze of griffins, candelabra, and acanthus buried halfway to the roof in mud. It is to see that temple turned to the Church of San Lorenzo in Miranda, with its once front door now opening 10 meters above the paths of the Forum.

Lorenzo was an early martyr for the church, persecuted by Valerian. Knowing he was about to be arrested, Lorenzo gathered all the church's wealth and distributed it to the poor, the maimed, the orphaned, and the leprous of Rome, even selling the sacred vessels to increase his offering. When Valerian demanded that Lorenzo deliver to Rome the church's treasure, he showed up with his motley entourage, saying, "Here. This is the wealth of the church." For this, he was grilled alive on a gridiron on the steps of the temple that became his church and he called out halfway through the torture, "It is well done, turn me over."

§

My city, the small city I call home now, sits in a soft pitch of land that slopes out of the Longfellow Mountains and into the roll of small hills dropping finally into the Atlantic in a web of islands and bays and rivers and stones. Alder thickets rope the creeks that descend from the mountains and they dig their roots deep into the gaping, sand-and-stone soil. Heavy sand blows up in the spring and fall when the winds rise and the air is alive with movement. It is a decent kind of life, this small town, and safe; a last outpost mentality I think, although it is far from being such. There are places father gone, more abandoned by the world, where the county highways that once brought traffic and commerce now carry only truckers running the back roads in billowing sacks of wind.

There is a man who lives west of my town, near a disheveled Christian youth camp draped across a low rise above the bracken-filled bogs of dead and dying trees; the old bed for the railroad track now pulled up and turned to a trail for snow machines and ATVs. This man still makes delicious milkshakes by hand. When I kick open the stuck door to his store with the toe of my boot, he looks up from a band saw where he is slicing a side of beef into steaks—agriculture meets industry. He uses the same saw to cut his lumber. Sawdust collects in the corners of the store. It sops up the running blood.

§

Once again I have returned to try and make sense of it, to piece fact and impression into a larger whole. But once again, I can only get so close. My heart beats effectively now, freed of its obstruction—blood moves smoothly through the delta of my lungs and the riverine ecosystem inside me flows free—but I still carry that mutation. The code of my existence is still written in error, but the consequences of that error have been removed by the careful hands of my surgeon, edited out like an errant paragraph from a book. The blood plunges through the eternal night inside my chest like the Six Mile churning and churning in the Alaska dusk and my own personal Suck Rock that once jutted out into current has been detonated and the pieces pulled from the river.

The body is of course our ultimate metaphor for most things, but particularly for the land. We get out into virgin country. We cross the shoulders of mountains, follow arterial rivers. We live in our own neck of the woods. The body is a metaphor for the built environment, too. Tunnels and sewers act as the bowels of the city. The veins of highways snake into the nucleus of the old town, and the city pulses with life. Then we come to the heart of things, which is most often not an actual building or even a park. The heart of the metropolis is both a place and a sense of place at the same time, an absent presence, a gathering of people, an area that fills with life and then empties again. Its purpose is the heart's purpose, this emptiness that fills and expels, over and over again, pulsing, always pulsing, with the lifeblood of commerce and commotion. We are inside the heart even as we are a part of it, as we move through the city; we are its blood and its muscle, its waste and its nourishing.

And because these metaphors are about our attention—as we get closer to the body, to the white, unblinking center of all that is us, to that piece of us and not us that is both actor and acted-upon by the world—we have to revert to a language of scale. But the closer we get, the slipperier our language gets. Like Mandelbrot measuring the coastline of Great Britain, the tools we use (the only tools we have) grow less and less useful as we descend, always descend, and fail to arrive at our intended destination. We get smaller as we get closer to the center of our narratives. The nearer I arrive the less I can describe and then suddenly all that remains is the ghost of the landscape. The narrative spins away from the central moment of the story, and I am left with fragments, images. That diamond of space opened by two hands. My still, unbeating heart packed in ice like a fish in the public market. The alternating breezes—the *hush* and *hiss*—of the ventilator that sound like the wind in the sky above my town. My cold body spread out beneath blue sheets like I am the city itself draped by the sky.

§

At every turn in Rome there lies a buried narrative, a memory, most of them violent and bloody, bearing the weight of tragedy and pathos. I write these words in a courtyard of orange trees with the stepping-stone buildings rising above me and scaffolded with laundry. To walk Rome is to descend into a living catacomb—it is a suitcase of bones and a basket of riches and blood. To write it is to descend into memory and this memory is far larger than my own. Layer by layer, like sinking into sediment and stone, one who reads this writing descends into my memories and into the memories of a culture as if into a canyon where the strata line up to meet the eye, some thick and speckled with obvious wealth, others paltry and thin. But then again, even inside the thinnest of layers there lies a richness that extends into the depths of the culture. Each memory tied to a place is tethered to all the lives lived in that space—a realization at once comforting and terrifying. Comforting in that, by knowing more, I find myself much more grounded in this landscape; terrifying since I will never know enough, no one will ever know enough, and we will continue to lose the world and slip through on reproductions.

The act of writing, as a descent into the catacomb of the self as it approaches the moment of vanishing, echoes the condition of memory where everything is lost yet still remains. Conversely, the work of ordering language—music and the demands of craft—creates the architecture in which words hang in that charged field between the thing and the thought, giving us *the electricity of both rather than the vertigo of neither.* The work anchors the writer outside the pure labyrinth of the mind, because language lives partially outside of the mind. Words are thing and not-thing; they are concrete and abstract at once. Language lives in the formation of metaphor as it combines the richness of the physical world with the structure of thinking—a quetzal in the shadow-forest of the mind.

Metaphor is that turn, the description that is not description, that undertaking that Plato tells us is possible for mere humans as we ape the gods. Metaphor is a radical statement of surprising equality, the moment when the writer says, despite all logic and sense, that one thing *is* another. Not one thing *resembles* another, although it does, but that one thing *is* another. But of course that's not quite true. Metaphor is the lie that tells us the deeper truth. Metaphor is the moment of connection that ties the world together, or perhaps, to say it another way, reveals the ties that are already there, lying hidden beneath the surface of the world, *hitched to everything else in the Universe.* Metaphor is the image that is *more than* image, the moment when, upon looking at that *other dark*—at the *missing* and the *unknown,* the *unknowable* and the *unsayable*—the writer's eyes turn away toward the known and the knowable world, our world. Towards these totems of our fragile world. Away from the white, unblinking center of it all, towards ants, quetzals, towers, and cathedrals. Towards rivers, mountains, and birds. Towards an unbeating heart.

§

His name is Mr. Baumgartner; his friends call him Bummie. The steaks Bummie cuts are rich and magenta, marled with pearled fat. The band saw stretches almost to the ceiling. It is pea green, like the refrigerator of a college apartment. He turns his back and bends to his work. The machine hums, the blade running in frightening arcs. He pushes the slick white haunch towards the blade.

I ask for a milkshake and he moves to the cooler and digs into the ice cream, its soft, cold mass, with thick forearms. When he bends down, I can see the sweat on his balding pate, his thinning hair patched gray and silver. He spoons the ice cream into an unclean blender. Actually, it is not unclean, it just looks that way, frosted from so many uses like glass out of the ocean. He adds milk and vanilla, a small cap of ground nutmeg. I look at his hands and realize he hasn't washed them to make this shake. I can see them clearly flecked with blood and smeared with congealed fat. There is blood on the rim of the half-gallon, the scoop. What he gives me tastes like a perfect kiss.

As I pass the afternoon at the counter, grading and reading and watching the sky, the regulars come in. I do not count myself among them, although I come here often. I am still new—the place working its touch on me. There's no sense that I belong to the land the way these men do, their families buried in rows beyond the treeline. I want that sensation, but what I feel is different. A space to move into, an opening of wind and air and light. And a flush of unoccupied distance. They come in and help themselves to coffee, their high rubber boots flared at the calf. Gimmecaps in garish green and orange. They speak in a common language, a language of names and places long familiar—Temple Stream, the Selridge farm, Franklin County—one I follow as if from a distance. It is like a foreign language I don't know too well, one I know by ear but still cannot speak.

On the road home, the still-life of a gray barn beyond low white hills, blown with snow, and a redtail high in the bare maple. Another carving huge turns in the brilliant air. The corduroy fallow and a sense of loss burned deep into the stone fence line running up into the reforested hills. Sometimes, late afternoons in the winter, when I drive out as the sun hangs low in the west a long time and the clouds are just right, I can be surrounded by mountains and sunset. Perhaps it is in these moments when the cobalt sky touches the stalk-clumped fields, when there's a distant sense of snow in the air, and the earth glows with a generous indigo that is really the absence of light below and its presence above, perhaps then this place becomes all places in a contourless land—the velvet glow of the earth and sky blending beneath the wind—and the world loses its texture as dusk reaches out to encircle the horizon.

XV.

After Rome, twenty years ago, we stumbled into Riomaggiore (the southernmost town of the *Cinque Terre*) on a tip from someone with whom we'd been traveling. After Rome, after the heat and the chaos (*bella Roma, bella chaos*), we lurched off the train still deep in the tunnel punched through the mountainside and emerged in the unanimous light of the town station. Narrow, carless streets dropping down toward the water or climbing up into the soft, dove-colored hills. Donna Anna Marie greeted us, her short, potato-sack body chuffing over, and called out, "Ciao, Bellos!" We had never spoken before, but she swept us up in huge hugs and directed us to a dorm in an old apartment—thirty bunk beds in a room built for ten. It was cheap and she was charming, plus there was a kitchen on the roof with a view to the water. And that's what we wanted. The Mediterranean. We changed clothes and almost ran for the beach that really wasn't a beach, just boulders tumbled down to the shore where we dove into the jade water, warm as weak tea, and hauled ourselves out onto the rocks like seals to bake in the sun.

§

The *Cinque Terre*. Five small villages rushing down in a tumble of stacked homes to meet the Gulf of Genoa and the Ligurian Sea. Plaster in tones of clay and sand and brick, balconies adorned with canvasses of drying laundry, and the narrow alleys that climb into the hills beyond, olive trees and family vineyards, stone walls and the smell of lavender and sunlight and dust. Nets beneath the olive trees and terraces overlooking the sea that wavers out beyond the shore.

Hard to get to, these villages are mainly accessible by train and by foot—there are roads, but they wind for miles inland before connecting to the highway system. The trains plow through the hills in long, dripping tunnels that occasionally break open to give a glimpse of the shore, a rocky beach far below or the small scallop of a jade-blue cove. The footpaths, where I am today hiking with Jennifer and my son, climb up into the hills above the shore. They echo a past as old as the towns. They carried people for thousands of years back and forth across the landscape through the stone-walled alleys and back streets, into the terraced vineyards and groves of stone pine (for the pesto). These trails are almost memory written physically onto the landscape, branching off like synapses into the mind of the hills. The hum of bees in the air bright as thought.

§

It was on this beach that is not a beach that Tony would meet the woman he would go on to marry—a woman from Denmark traveling alone on vacation. While Tony was occupied with her, I was left to myself and spent almost a week making friends for a day or two and then losing them as they would depart again on the train. The Europe of my youth was like that then: a time of transitory people, of relationships that lasted days, or less, but felt as intense as many I have had since. It was the intimacy of sleeping side-by-side with strangers, of feeling at once isolated (from the language, from the culture) and perfectly at home with those fellow travelers likewise cut off.

One day, I met a chef-in-training at the *Cordon Bleu* (with wild tangles of blond curls and a name I can no longer recall). She and I walked the markets and ate wildly good food. I tasted pesto for the first time on her recommendation in a small bistro above the water. When the plates came, a mound of pasta with a rather surprising gobbet of green right in the center; it was exquisite, like concentrated summer, deep and green and full in the mouth (god, I can almost taste it now), made in the kitchen from pine nuts, basil, olive oil, garlic, and Parmesan all grown within that valley. We ordered second helpings and cleaned both plates. Then we walked up the hillsides and she pulled out a small pipe and foil pouch of Moroccan hashish. We smoked as the sun set into the Mediterranean and the world glowed with promise and a cloudy warmth that echoed the fading sky.

§

When I recall these moments of the past, I am trying to take fragments of my life and fix them in place. I am trying to corral my life and make it readable. I am trying to make it beautiful. Beauty attempts to hold static what cannot remain so, and of course it doesn't remain. The world flexes and moves, altering and changing day by day. Beauty is a violence imposed on time because it attempts to hold motionless what cannot be held. In the act of creation, the world enters us and we change it, tame it, make it portable; this is what Kant says, if you remember. We would be overwhelmed by the world, by the Italian hill country come down here to meet the shore and the silk of the blue sky above the Mediterranean, its plentitude and picturesque wealth, if we could refrain from subjugating it, if only for a short time. Art and poetry and history—the city itself—they all take on the experience of the world, the physical acreage of place and experience, of cornfield and of rainforest, of ancient trail through a hillside of stone and olive trees, and transmute it to a comprehensible gloss. Such renovation cannot hold. Beauty ossifies like language and turns fossil, and we get by on reproductions. This is a process at once tragic and necessary. We lose because we cannot do otherwise. We lose what we thought we knew—a gathering of larks beneath the window, the weight of wine like meat on our tongues.

§

After my chef-friend hopped back on a train, headed back to her training in Paris or Bonn or somewhere else, I found a group of Californian girls who wanted company and we sunned and drank and got up at dawn to swim in the sea. A local fishermen, Paolo, took a shine to the girls and took us all out in his fishing boat, a small 14-foot outboard painted the blue of the Virgin Mary. I remember Paolo as almost a caricature— lazy curls of dark hair under a blue fisherman's cap, shirt open, an easy smile and broken English. We motored out to an isolated cove with black-headed gulls churning behind us in a froth, lured by the possibility of fish. We anchored and Paolo motioned for us to dive in. We all did, quickly. The water warm and silken. The sky a towering archway. I lay with my head back in the clarity of that topaz water like I was floating in and among the fountains of the sky. As if the sky had bent down and lifted me into its heart. I was nowhere and everywhere at once. The sea stretched out to the west and the chalky, sunbaked hills climbed up to the east and the world felt infinite and wet with promise.

Back in the boat, drying off in the powerful sun, one girl told the rest of us that she saw an octopus down below. When Paolo heard the word, he blurted out, *"Polpo!"* grabbed his mask and dove over the side. He reappeared minutes later, grinning and dripping, with a sizeable octopus, a mottle of gray and green and brown in his hand, the tentacles working against the streaming muscles of his arm. He cooked it that night on the terrace of our hostel. The soft light of sunset roaming all along the coast, the wine cold and brusque and cheap, and Paolo flipping the octopus back and again on the gridiron, tentacles slapping, until it was charred and broken on the outside but still sweet and tender, dripping with a sauce of lemon and garlic and parsley. Oh, oh, oh…

§

I talked earlier about beauty, the form of it, and the way the mind cajoles the world into form. That's what Kant says, at least, and it makes sense to me. Beauty is what we make from the world—it is a human construction, delicate and fragile that needs to be continually renewed. The quetzal, the pelican, the harbor in Riomaggiore. But Kant talks about something else, too. That moment when the power of the world, its abundance and potential for violence—like the possible road running out before the mind forever when it considers infinity—when the world tries to break the mind, tries to limit it. But, of course, the world does no such thing. It doesn't *try* to do anything. It just exists. Its realities—like the coast of Britain, like the number of beetles occupying one tree in Monte

Verde, like a mountain choked in mist falling away in all directions—are bigger than the mind's powers to control the world and make it beautiful. The world and its particulars overflow our senses and our attempts to create a form from them. The abundance of the world is often more than the mind can handle, and at that moment of overwhelming the thinking self is thrown back on itself and forced to confront its own impotence. Kant calls this moment the sublime, and for him it exists in the awesome, in the might and power of nature when the world seems to turn against us: the towering cliff, the boil of storm clouds and the rash winds of the hurricane, the mountain cliff climbing high above the weary traveler.

But the world has other powers. The power of the sublime need not be gargantuan and threatening; it need not be larger than life, because, quite honestly, our lives are so fragile. It need only be a hidden hive of wasps in a nurse log dropped across a trail in the forever twilight of the rainforest. Or a plunging curtain of river water falling 5 feet into a pool it carved from the bedrock. It need only be 4 grams of muscle blocking the flow of blood from a heart. The sublime, too, can be found in the human world, in the sweep of history layered deep into the black stones of *Santa Maria de Trastevere*. In long walls of bone, deep beneath the architecture of light that is Paris. The finite self cast against the stretched arc of our very human past. The forces that bend the human subject to their will reduce us to an infinite trifling, a fragile sack of bone and mind that (sometimes) overcomes its frailty to reach up and make a mark on the great wall of time.

If beauty lives in the moment when we make the world subject to us, then the sublime is its opposite. The sublime, then, is the moment when the mind, the self, the body, that sense of ME, when they are—one and all—made subject to the world, and then, something magical happens. In that moment the power of the mind reaches beyond all bounds. The sublime is the moment when, once made subject to the power of the world and our own frailty, the imagination rises beyond the limits of the physical world and encompasses the physical world that would make it a subject. That moment is a kind of magic. That moment is art. That moment is metaphor. The mind takes the potency of the world—its incomprehensible strength and might: whether that is God or the Soul or Nature or Death—and turns it into something comprehensible, something that will echo in the mind of another person perhaps hundreds of years from now, like a gong long struck and resounding.

Metaphor says that the world is liquid and the mind can make the forms of the world flow in directions impossible. Metaphor opens the door to the infinite and the omnipotent. It defines the world anew under boundaries drawn only by the imagination. Metaphor is that moment when the mind overcomes the physical limits of the body and the world and reaches into the infinite dream of the sky. The moment of the sublime—of metaphor—should be a kind of victory, but instead it feels like tragedy. The tragedy is that in the very act of metaphor we speak of both overcoming and succumbing to the very limitations that drive us to overcome in the first place. We are fragile beings, chemical sparks that have found a way to live beyond our tiny lives. We have the opportunity that Achilles dreamed of—to be remembered—to say something that will echo down the hallway of time and fill the minds of readers not yet born. But to seize this opportunity is to acknowledge our fragility inside this world of depth and splendor, of city and forest, of beach and farm, to find beauty in a world of transience and brevity, and to try and hold these moments of meaning still. The tragedy is not that these moments are rare; it is that they rarely last. Our metaphors die. Metaphors are fragile—not the way the body is fragile—but the way species are fragile. They spring forth and last for as long as they are adapted to their environment, and then they perish. Some live on like fossils, like fossilized thought, like ghosts in the machine that is language. A few, like scientific metaphors, become so central to our thinking that we cannot, in fact, think without them. A few, a tiny few, a small sampling of the great cacophony of language that rises up from the human species, survive. But most perish. Then the process begins again.

§

We ended the night those twenty years ago up the coast, by boat again, me and the girls from California, in a bar overlooking the harbor of Vernazza, the fourth town going north. The stars were a lush bramble in the sky and the night was warm, the wine clean and cold, and it was easy to believe that this would be the rest of my life, that such moments would never fade and I would be young forever and forever able to move about the world as if free from the past—and even the present, really—as only one person I knew in the whole world had any idea where I was and what I was doing, and he, quite frankly, didn't care.

The hills beyond us glowed—slightly—with the lights of Genoa and the wine-dark sea splashed against the rocks below us with its cautious applause. The world was ancient and new and made for us again. We ate and drank and laughed and sang in many languages that became one and the world spun around us like we were its focal point. And we were.

We returned from Vernazza with the water spraying into our faces from the chuff of the bow smacking the waves. Our boat pulled into the town the way a blessing of rain muscles through the trees in the heat of the day, with only a few lights speckled up the sides of the dark hills. The bakers were at work and the town smelled of bread and yeast and in the sudden quiet full of ticking as the boat pulled to the dock, warmth rising to the thin spackle of stars, we bought hot bread and tore it apart in the dark.

§

Once again I survived. Once again I have returned to hold this tale out toward you. But that's not the end. My heart beats cleanly inside my chest and my blood flows free, but I am not the only one in this story. This disease is written into the architecture of who I am. It is carried in the very instructions that made me, in the code. And there's another one who carries that code. My son. *My son is my elegy, waiting to be written.* I wrote those words long ago, before I knew the truth, and yet I meant them. Even then. In every parent there is fear for the future. Fear is what we carry with us, its gauzy weight, along with our love and our pride. I wrote those words long ago, but that was before. My fear was general and undefined, based on the darker narratives of the world. It lived on the edges of my vision and, yes, lurked in my dreams. But now I have to consider a much more concrete and actual fear: that I may have passed this error on to him. He has been examined and his heart is clear and healthy. But that's now. My symptoms showed up late in my life and I have wondered why, why I didn't just collapse, like so many other young athletes. It could have happened anytime. My disease is the most common cause of sudden cardiac death in people under age 30. At any time it could have happened. As a young man playing football or rugby, running wind sprints or gassers across the hot, dry grass of late summer till the blood pounded in my temples and throbbed behind my eyes. Or on my climb up to the top of *Cerro de la Muerte*, in the fifth or sixth hour of riding upwards, always upwards, as I stood on the pedals, doubled over the handlebars, and heaved with breath, my heart banging away in my chest.

In the days after my surgery, lying in that white room with the sunlight reflecting off the skyscraper across the city, among the wires and catheters snaking out from me to the various machines gathered around me like concerned friends, I asked my surgeon, Why? *Why now? Why did this happen so late in my life? Why didn't I die young?*

He looked at me with his sad confidence—this small man of amazing talent and poise, his silver hair curled back on his head and his skin the color of *café con leche*—he looked at me, and all he could tell me was this: "It's a dynamic disease." *Dynamic.* That's the word that stayed with me. At first that word seemed shorthand for, *we don't know.* A way of evading that absence, that lack of knowledge. He is a brilliant surgeon and a smart man. He didn't want to admit that gap in his world. He couldn't say it that way: *we just don't know.* But now I think that word is far more complicated than simple ignorance. Life is dynamic. So is the world. Life is a cacophony of facts. A flow of data that crashes down and over us, a spume of information that finds, perhaps, a ghostly kind of order that holds for a moment there inside the chaos. Life changes and despite our efforts to simplify existence and make our lives safe and comprehensible, we cannot—finally—accomplish our goals. That seems like an easy and obvious conclusion, but like almost everything obvious there are layers beyond the surface. There are complications.

My son may carry the disease. Or he may not. But even if he has that code written into him, that typo down deep in the blueprint of his body, he may not develop any symptoms. No one knows. *It's a dynamic disease.* Maybe he will have to have my surgery later in life. I hope not. Maybe something worse will happen. Right now he is safe and growing into a man to be proud of. He is alive in the moment and that moment forever slips away from me fading into a past I create and am created by. He is safe and terribly at risk. *My son is my elegy.* That sentence cuts both ways. One or the other is inevitable, and both are unthinkable.

Today, in Italy's hill country come down to kneel between the thighs of the sea, that small dinghy cuts forever across the striped lights of Riomaggiore, their dazzle drizzled onto the bronze flank of the dark. The boat chuffs into the harbor again and again in my mind, roads rising into a *purgatorio* of windows shuttered against the night air. Carcasses of boats overturned on the docks. The gathering of cats coming down to the quay in hopes of fish. That night perfect and eternal in memory. It's all here, in pieces perhaps, but that's all I have: pieces. The gilded dark, trains tearing at the hillsides with their oil-stained whistles. The smell of the bread. Stars turning wheels above our heads.

§

Twenty years later, I am back in Vernazza wading hip deep in memory. The tower bar's still there, but now it's ramped up to a high-end restaurant where we eat one night: hard goat cheese and parmesan, local honey as clear as glass and tasting of sage and wild clover, and, you guessed it, octopus in lemon and oil over radicchio. The narrow streets of saffron and brick still wind their way into the vineyards, the train still clanks through the hills above the small, jade pool of the harbor.

This is a landscape where little has changed—on purpose. The people of Italy in general, and of the *Cinque Terre* specifically, have worked hard to keep this area unchanged—refusing offers from the national government to widen and develop the roads that connect the villages to the inland highways, roads that weren't built until the 1960s. These refusals represent an attempt to hold on to culture and memory, to hold back the forces of modernization and upheaval that plow over the past and bury it in convenience and sameness, efforts to dismiss history (these villages were built onto the cliffs as they were to repel the pirates that cruised the Mediterranean a thousand years ago) and move toward uniformity.

Such efforts are also what attract tourists, tourists like me and my family, I admit, and during the day the towns fill up, especially when the water taxi that runs the coastline arrives at the small stone pier near the harbor, letting loose a thatch of Germans and Americans and Scandinavians who poke the snouts of their cameras into the alleys and sit at the tables overlooking the harbor with their polite glass of local wine and a half-assed pizza from the lousy restaurants lining the harbor. During the day the town feels like a stage set, like a preserved specimen under glass, like Lenin's corpse up for display in Red Square, an impossible attempt to hold on to the past, a past we consume as easily as food.

We spend most of our days hiking up into the hills, eating lunch at overlooked overlook-cafés where the owner is the cook and the waiter and the sliced tomatoes for the caprese are still warm from the sun and the mozzarella tastes like soft milk and butter. We sit and watch the clouds move across a glamorous sky and feel the wind climb the hills with its load of cypress and olive. The sun moves slowly in its terrible arc across the sky and I can feel time passing like a huge white ship crossing the Gulf of Genoa, a ship sailing to a new land forever green. But in the morning, before the boats arrive and the town is beginning to wake— the sun comes late to these valleys—and I walk the streets, after my *caffè con zucchero* at *Il Pirata*, gathering breakfast for my family, the bread still warm from the night ovens, strawberries brought down from the hills, and the lemons and the smell of basil, that's when I might be twenty again, although I rarely woke this early then. That's when time vanishes and memory becomes one with the moment and there is little to know except the space that I walk through, a space that carries its years effortlessly like a breeze. Or at night, in the tower restaurant, with a plate of cheese and wild honey clear as glass and tasting of clover and sunlight set before me—the tang of the hard goat cheese, the fruity parmesan, and a glass of the local *sciacchetrà*, cold and brusque and tasting a bit of the sea—when the crowds are gone and the wind picks up carrying the heat off our skin, the open ocean to one side and the harbor to the other, locals below taking their evening *passeggiata*, the murmur of greeting as they pass one another down to the boats and back again, toward the train station and beyond, along the river that cuts through the small farms and vineyards now slathered in the day's last apricot light, that's when the ghosts of past and present walk together, when something moves on the water that might be my mind and I am twenty-something and forty-something at the same time and the world doesn't wait for me to return.

Such moments never last, of course, and nothing I am saying here is new; this is age and the passage of time and the fear of death, but, as I said, there is more to this story than that. If memory is culture and culture is a bucket of blood we carry with us, then what these towns represent, what my efforts to hold back time represent, is an attempt to deny nature's full weight, which is life and death together. To be present and absent at once. It is to live in the past without grief sitting down at the table with me, with my heart beating safely and comfortably inside my chest. To have the cheese and the honey and the smell of the salt air in the blessed summer night without the fear, without the pain and all the bloodied bodies that make such ease possible. But then again, it is also to know a place incompletely and in fragments, to define a specimen under glass; Lenin again, that grotesque *memento mori*, perhaps, or a still-life of peaches the color of dawn and a bottle of wine and a knife.

CODA:

In Rome, the day before we left for the *Cinque Terre*, I borrowed a bike from the hotel and zipped down *Viale di Trastevere* and across the *Ponte Sublicio* to the Protestant Cemetery (literally *il Cimitero Acattolico*—the Non-Catholic Cemetery). The cemetery was built outside the wall, since non-Catholics could not be buried inside the Holy City and Jews had their own burial ground in Trastevere. Tall cypress and a profusion of flowers surround the graves and spill across the walls, the stones built above the ground and gathered close, and nearby the Pyramid of Cestius alongside a section of Rome's ancient Aurelian wall. I have come to see two graves—Keats' and Shelley's. Shelley's I find first, high, near the south wall—the flat sepulcher surrounded by boxwood and the lounging, arrogant cats. The flat stone is carved with Latin—*Cor Cordium,* or Heart of Hearts—and lines from *The Tempest.* This epitaph is Ariel consoling Ferdinand, the prince of Naples, after Ferdinand's father's apparent death by drowning:

> *Nothing of him that doth fade,*
> *But doth suffer a sea-change,*
> *Into something rich and strange*

Here is that human hope for permanence, that desire to exist beyond existence. Nothing fades but life changes. Like the tide it returns revised and reborn. It's all here. In metaphor, in the very landscape, at least. The cemetery is an oasis of the pastoral in the business of the urban world. It is loss defined but also a kind of longevity. Stretching out from the grave: umbrella pines, myrtle shrubs, roses, and carpets of wild violets. *It might make one in love with death, to think that one should be buried in so sweet a place,* wrote Shelley about the cemetery, not long before he drowned and his remains were placed there.

In 1822, in the Gulf of Spezzia, his schooner Ariel capsized and Shelley did drown. When his body washed ashore days later, Lord Byron, Edward Trelawney, and Leigh Hunt uncovered Shelley from where he had been lightly buried in the sand and cremated his body on the shore, surrounded by pillars of cypress and the wild blooms of the salt roses. They burned his body, pouring wine and oil and salt over him so that the flames glistened and quivered. When the fire died down, what remained were a few bones, ashes, and Shelley's heart, whole and unconsumed. Trelawney reached into the coals and pulled the heart out, scorching his hand badly in the process. Trelawney gave the heart to Hunt, who took it with some apparent reservation and finally gave it to Mary Shelley, who kept it until her death, wrapped in some of the pages of *Adonais*, Shelley's elegy for John Keats.

§

I keep trying. I return to the world and its particulars. I return to the ignorant eye to observe a sun—a *dynamic* sun—that remains both unknowable and known as it sparkles above the Gulf of Genoa. I hear the quetzal as it authors its mystical call into the misted oaks of the Savegre Valley and the harpy eagle as it haunts the distant edges of the Corcovado rainforest. The Eiffel Tower as it institutes itself above the flat pan of the Champs de Mars and the vortex of the Suck Hole as it spins and spins in the unending arctic light. Roads and watersheds as they drop off toward eternity from atop *Cerro de la Muerte*. The bones of the dead lie in rows deep below the earth like macabre fencing and the cities of the leaf-cutter ant glow silently beneath their mounds, lit by the labor of their millions of citizens. My heart beats precisely in my chest. My son. Each place, each metaphor, each story, each image, each memory made new, made into language, the unthinkable into thought. I turn back again and again, returning to the source with fresh words. Thus, loss is overcome through elegy and place saved through language. Almost.

§

Keats' tomb I find, at last, after turning back and again, losing my way among the small alleys of stones and cypress. The maze of the place is both confounding and wonderful. Like getting lost in a blooming garden of death. But finally I find it, Keats' grave. It lies near the pyramid and stands—a tall, weather-worn stone with a shoddy lyre carved on the top, surrounded by irises flying their bright flags of purple—but the marker is unnamed. Back in Rome, Keats knew he was going to die, and early, from the tuberculosis that ran through his family like a brush fire, killing first his mother and then his brother, Tom, and he said he wanted only the following written on his funeral stone:

Here lies One Whose Name was writ in Water.

His desired epitaph (more was ultimately carved into the stone, but that phrase is all that Keats wanted there) suggests the impermanence of all things. It suggests absence and dissolution. The water that carries his name swirling and flowing until everything is gone. It suggests the fading away of words, his words, his name. But I am not so sure he believed that, finally. One of Keats' last poems, "This Living Hand," written in full knowledge of his approaching death—he had nursed Tom and his mother long enough to know the signs—sets up a voice in opposition to his own, chosen epitaph:

> *This living hand, now warm and capable*
> *Of earnest grasping, would, if it were cold*
> *And in the icy silence of the tomb,*
> *So haunt thy days and chill thy dreaming nights*
> *That thou wouldst wish thine own heart dry of blood*
> *So in my veins red life might stream again,*
> *And thou be conscience-calmed—see here it is—*
> *I hold it towards you.*

This poem is an attack on the living by the almost dead, perhaps on his critics, perhaps on Fanny Brawne whom he may have believed unfaithful, but it also another kind of epitaph spoken directly to the reader so many years and centuries later. This hand represents something beyond what was carved into his tombstone; here the poet reaches from beyond the grave with the voice of memory and grief (which is, of course, a kind of memory) and asks you to make him live again, asks that you provide the blood that will rehabilitate him. You, the reader, are the maker. This new life cannot exist without the old, without Keats, of course, but equally it cannot exist without you to give it form and blood. The author and the reader. The world and the word. The hand, at the end, is it alive or dead? It is of course both; that's the negative capability of the poem, the duality of memory, since we keep alive through memory only what we have lost and what we grieve for. Memory and story revive what is gone, still, and silent. But memory is weak and subject to forces beyond its control, and story cannot last. Elegy cannot revive the dead. The blood never flows back into that hand, even as it is held out to us.

And yet, in some way, it does. Because here's the saving grace—that hand is also the poem, the story, the words. Keats holds it out to you from across the span of years. He works to defy death even as he fails, even as he coughs himself bloody in a small bed in a small room beside the Spanish Steps. He wants to live beyond his time, to be more than a name glimmering like light on the water, a fading thought, a passing star, bright as it might be. He wrote to Fanny earlier in his life: *I have lov'd the principle of beauty in all things, and if I had had time I would have made myself remember'd.* In this final poem, his last gesture to the living world that will of course outlast him, he reaches out to the readers of the future, to the potential of time that drives ever onward, with a beautiful gift. Something remains, he tells us, something exists because it has been said. Some fragment endures in the substance of loss. Some pulse travels through us from a heart that once beat. Some echo can be heard of what was once sung.

Hopefully that is enough: the world, the word. The memory, the echo. The mountain, the sun, the city. The rocks, the ants, the river, the bird. *Cor Cordium.* Hopefully that is enough. My heart held out in a hand burned by the fire. See? Here it is. I hold it towards you.

Further Reading

Abbey, Edward. *Desert Solitaire: A Season in the Wilderness.*
    New York: Simon & Schuster, 1990.
Beachy-Quick, Dan. *Wonderful Investigations: Essays,
    Meditations, Tales.* Minneapolis: Milkweed,
    2012.
Benjamin, Walter. *Selected Writings.* Translated by Howard
    Eiland and Michael William Jennings. Cambridge,
    MA: Belknap of Harvard UP, 2003.
Beletsky, Les. *Costa Rica: The Ecotravellers' Wildlife Guide.* San
    Diego: Academic Press, 1998.
Bishop, Elizabeth. *The Collected Poems of Elizabeth Bishop.*
    New York: Farrar, Strauss and Giroux, 1969.
-----. *One Art: Letters Selected and Edited.* Edited by Robert
    Giroux. New York: The Noonday Press, 1994.
Chatwin, Bruce. *The Songlines.* New York: Viking, 1987.
Crèvecoeur, Michel-Guillaume Jean. *Letters from an American
    Farmer.* Teddington: Echo Library, 2006.
Dante, Alighieri. *Dante's Inferno: the First Part of the Divine
    Comedy of Dante Alighieri.* Translated by Tom Phillips.
    New York: Thames and Hudson, 1985.
Davidson, Chad. *Consolation Miracle.* Carbondale: Southern
    Illinois UP, 2003.
Derrida, Jacques. *Writing and Difference.* Translated by Alan
    Bass. Chicago: The University of Chicago Press, 1978.
Dillard, Annie. *Pilgrim at Tinker Creek.* New York: Harper &
    Row, 1985.
Emerson, Ralph W. *Selections from Ralph Waldo Emerson.*
    Edited by Stephen E. Whicher. Boston: Houghton
    Mifflin, 1960.
Foucault, Michel. *Death and the Labyrinth.* Translated by
    Charles Ruas. New York: Vintage, 1986.

Heidegger, Martin. *Poetry, Language, Thought.* Translated by
    Albert Hofstader. New York: Harper & Row, 1971.
-----. *What is Called Thinking?* Translated by Fred D.
    Wieck and J. Glenn Gray. New York: Harper &
    Row, 1969.
Homer. *The Iliad.* Translated by Robert Fagles. New
    York: Viking, 1990.
Gilbert, Jack. *The Great Fires.* New York: Knopf, 1996.
Gleick, James. *Chaos: Making a New Science.* New York:
    Vintage, 1997.
Keats, John. *Complete Poems and Selected Letters of John
    Keats.* New York: Modern Library, 2001.
Kövecses, Zoltán. *Metaphor: a Practical Introduction.*
    New York: Oxford UP, 2002.
Lakoff, George, and Mark Johnson. *Metaphors We Live
    By.* Chicago: University of Chicago, 2003.
Leopold, Aldo. *A Sand Count Almanac and Sketches
    Here and There.* New York: Oxford UP, 1968.
Levis, Larry. *The Gazer Within.* Ann Arbor: University
    of Michigan, 2001.
-----. *The Widening Spell of the Leaves.* Pittsburgh:
    University of Pittsburgh, 1991.
Lopez, Barry. *Crossing Open Ground.* New York:
    Vintage, 1989.
Matthiessen, Peter. *The Snow Leopard.* New York:
    Penguin, 1996.
McFague, Sallie. *Metaphorical Theology: Models of God
    in Religious Language.* Fortress Press:
    Philadelphia, 1982.
McHugh, Heather. *Broken English: Poetry and
    Partiality.* Wesleyan University Press: Hanover,
    1993.
Milton, John. *John Milton: Selected Poems.*
    London: Penguin, 2007.
The New English Bible with the Apocrypha. New York: Oxford
    UP, 1971.
Muir, John. *My First Summer in the Sierras.* New York:
    Penguin, 1987.
Nietzsche, Friedrich. *The Gay Science.* Translated by Walter
    Kaufmann. New York: Vintage, 1974.

Pinker, Steven. *The Stuff of Thought: Language as a Window into Human Nature*. New York: Viking, 2007.

Plato, *Phaedrus and Letters VII and VIII*. Translated by Walter Hamilton. New York: Penguin, 1973.

-----. *Symposium*. Translated by Alexander Nehamas and Paul Woodruff. Indianapolis: Hackett Pub. 1989.

-----. *Princeton Encyclopedia of Poetry and Poetics*. Edited by Alex Preminger and T.V.F. Brogan. Princeton: Princeton UP, 1993.

Ramazani, Jahan. *The Poetry of Mourning: The Modern Elegy from Hardy to Heaney*. Chicago: University of Chicago Press, 1994.

Sacks, Peter M. *The English Elegy: Studies in the Genre from Spenser to Yeats*. Baltimore: Johns Hopkins UP, 1985.

Shakespeare, William. *The Riverside Shakespeare: The Complete Works*. Edited by G. Blakemore Evans and J. J. M. Tobin. Boston: Houghton Mifflin, 1997.

Solnit, Rebecca. *Wanderlust: A History of Walking*. New York: Penguin, 2001.

Stevens, Wallace. *The Collected Poems*. New York: Vintage, 1982.

-----. *Opus Posthumous*. Edited by Milton J. Bates. New York: Vintage:, 1990.

Stiles, F. Gary; Skutch, Alexander F. *A Guide to the Birds of Costa Rica*. Ithaca: Comstock, 1989.

Thoreau, Henry David. *Henry D. Thoreau: Journal*. Princeton: Princeton UP, 1997.
-----. *Walden*. Edited by J. Lyndon Shanley. Princeton: Princeton UP, 1971.

Turner, Jack. *The Abstract Wild*. Tucson: University of Arizona Press, 1997.

Walcott, Derek. *Midsummer*. New York: The Noonday Press, 1984.

-----. *Omeros*. New York: Farrar Straus Giroux, 1990.

Wallace, Alfred Russell. *The Malay Archipelago: The Land of the Orang-utan and the Bird of Paradise*. Singapore: Oxford UP, 1991.

Wilson, Edward O. *Biophilia*. Cambridge, MA: Harvard UP, 1984.